Advance Praise for *Gandhi and the Unspeakable*

"History occasionally witnesses struggles between the forces of life and forces of death where every defeat of the latter reinforces the faith in the ultimate triumph of truth over untruth while every success of the latter contains the possibility of humanity's total destruction. Jim Douglass's deeply researched little masterpiece based on Gandhi's faith in non-violence and his assassins' misguided philosophy is an eloquent story of the two conflicting philosophies that humankind faces today and makes us pause and think."
—**Narayan Desai**, author, *My Life is My Message*

"This book is truly a search for the Truth. There is more to Gandhi's assassination than has been revealed. This book is well argued, documented and very revealing."   —**Arun Gandhi**, President, Gandhi Worldwide Education Institute, Rochester, New York

"Just as he did with the life and death of John F. Kennedy, author and activist Jim Douglass has meticulously examined the final days and death of Mahatma Gandhi to find out why he was killed. In doing so, Douglass sheds new light on the power of nonviolence in the face of the Unspeakable. This book deepens our own understanding of nonviolence, and encourages us to go forward, like Gandhi, in faith, hope, love, and truth to confront the Unspeakable today."
—**John Dear**, editor, *Mohandas Gandhi: Essential Writings*

"This is an extraordinarily shocking study of the complicity of India's established political order with Gandhi's assassins that is at once deeply disturbing and profoundly illuminating. James Douglass is one of the few persons on the planet with the intellectual and experiential credentials to explore this long neglected, yet essential, dimension of Gandhi's life and death. He grasps the connections with a similar complicity of comparable dark and hidden forces in several American assassinations during the 1960s that unleashed a surge of negative energy that has not diminished with time. Douglass makes brilliant use of Thomas Merton's concept of the 'Unspeakable' to situate these happenings where they ultimately belong—beyond analysis and narration in the realm of lethal metaphor."   —**Richard Falk**, Milbank Professor of International Law Emeritus, Princeton University

"The book tells in effect two stories: the rise of Gandhi, and the stirring up of dark forces against him. The first story should be familiar to many of us, but even I, who have made a lifelong study of Gandhi, learned much from Douglass's perspective—with such passion and perceptiveness is it written. The second story left me shaken, as of course it should. If we do not break through the cognitive dissonance that leads some of us to deny the depth of the evil Douglass has exposed, if we do not say 'never again' to these atrocities and set ourselves on a course to make them impossible from now on, God help us."
—**Michael Nagler**, Metta Center

"Jim Douglass counterposes the deadly machinations of Gandhi's probable killers with the incredible bravery of Gandhi and his followers; the one group scheming violence in secret while Gandhi repeatedly risked all employing the incredible power of transparency and nonviolence. It is a lesson to us in these times of night raids and drone assassinations, of the imperishable power of courage and truth, if we ourselves strive to combine them. I heartily recommend this book."
—**Kathy Kelly,**
Voices for Creative Nonviolence

"Illuminated by research and studded with anguish, this dramatic text is a source of hope." —**Rajmohan Gandhi,** Research Professor,
University of Illinois at Urbana-Champaign,
and biographer of his grandfather, Mahatma Gandhi

"In this brilliant and disturbing book, James Douglass exposes the 'Unspeakable' truth about Gandhi's assassination: the complicity of corporate and government power in the attempt to kill not just the man but the vision. But for the reader of this book the vision becomes a challenge once more as we encounter Gandhi even at the final moment looking on his killer with love. A powerful spiritual experience. —**Bishop Thomas J. Gumbleton**

"James Douglass examines with admirable diligence and sensitivity Gandhi's final experiment with truth, which transformed his assassination into the end of a catastrophic civil war, calling a mass slaughter to a halt. Douglass has wisely focused our attention on a key classic moment, bringing it compellingly into our consciousness." —**Dennis Dalton,** Professor Emeritus
of Political Science, Barnard College, Columbia University,
and author of *Mahatma Gandhi. Nonviolent Power in Action*

"James W. Douglass's book on the assassination of President John F. Kennedy was, hands down, one of the most riveting books I have ever read: it quite literally kept me up at night, as I pored over his meticulous presentation of the case. Now, in his new book, Douglass looks at the assassination of the 20th century's 'Great Soul,' and, in the process, raises serious questions about power, violence, and sin. A necessary book about a necessary human being."
—**James Martin, SJ,** author, *My Life with the Saints*

"In his fascinating reconstruction of the events leading to Gandhi's assassination, Jim Douglass brings us significant information and new perspectives. These are vital to our understanding of that tragedy and also of its implications for today's world. Set in a larger context, Douglass's account of the extreme nationalism and fundamentalism that motivated his assassination sheds light on comparable forces tearing at our world today. As Gandhi could have predicted, violence escalates, assassination tactics spin out of control, terrorism feeds off itself, be it by the state or insurgents. To help us find our way, the kind of knowledge Douglass gives us is essential." —**Joanna Macy,** author,
*World as Lover, World as Self: Courage
for Global Justice and Ecological Renewal*

GANDHI and the UNSPEAKABLE

GANDHI and the UNSPEAKABLE

His Final Experiment with Truth

James W. Douglass

ORBIS BOOKS
Maryknoll, New York 10545

Manufactured in the United States of America

Library of Congress Cataloging-in-Publication Data

Douglass, James W.
    Gandhi and the unspeakable : his final experiment with truth /
James W. Douglass.
        p. cm.
    Includes bibliographical references and index.
    ISBN 978-1-57075-963-5 (cloth); eISBN 978-1-60833-107-9
    1. Gandhi, Mahatma, 1869-1948. 2. Gandhi, Mahatma, 1869-
1948—Assassination. 3. Gandhi, Mahatma, 1869-1948—Philosophy.
4. Statesmen—India—Biography. 5. Pacifists—India—Biography.
6. India—Politics and government—1919-1947. I. Title.
DS481.G3D66 2012
954.03'5092—dc23
[B]

To Rick Ambrose,

who lived the truths he believed.

Pray for us.

Contents

Introduction

I never planned to write a book about Gandhi. I had even passed on my Gandhi library to a friend, Jonathan Wilson-Hartgrove, encouraging him to write a book on Gandhi. Unasked, Jonathan suddenly returned all the Gandhi books, as if he knew I would need them. Then, as I visited another friend, John Dear, at his New Mexico hermitage, it was as if Gandhi walked in from the desert.

John said he had learned from our mutual friend, Arun Gandhi, that Arun's grandfather, Mohandas Gandhi, was assassinated by a powerful conspiracy that involved Indian government complicity.[1] If that was so, I realized it meant a parallel between Gandhi's murder and the plots to kill Martin Luther King and Malcolm X that I was researching for a book. Might Gandhi's martyrdom be a way into the stories of Martin and Malcolm?

Gandhi's autobiography had taught me the process of an "experiment with truth." His inherently surprising method—to go totally for the truth in one's life without set expectations—was now leading me from Martin and Malcolm back to the source of an experiment with truth, Gandhi himself. So it came to pass, in my struggle with a subterranean truth in a U.S. context, that I was drawn into the climactic truth of the nonviolent struggle in India.

Fifteen years ago, I began exploring the truth of four critical assassinations of the United States: those of John F. Kennedy, Martin Luther King, Jr., Malcolm X, and Robert F. Kennedy. They were all shot to death in four and a half years at the height of the 1960s, from the end of 1963 to the middle of 1968. Their murders in Dallas, Harlem, Memphis, and Los Angeles seemed to change forever the U.S. political and spiritual landscape, leaving nothing of democracy but the stage props. One thing that struck me while investigating the systemic killing of all four leaders was their underlying unity. That was true of both the men and their murders.

At first glance the Kennedys could hardly have been more different from King and Malcolm. John, a president, and Robert, a likely president-to-be, acted from very different points on the political and economic spectrum than did the dissenting prophets, Martin and Malcolm. The first two men were at the center of power; the latter two were near its periphery. Yet all four were agents of change whose murders revealed their unity at the heart of America. All four were trying to transform the center, and something in the center would not let them do it. The more I learned about their turning toward a hopeful future, the more I came to see their four stories as one story—or four dimensions of the same story. But it was a story that took one into the Unspeakable.

In the midst of the '60s, at the Abbey of Gethsemani in Kentucky, the great Trappist monk and writer Thomas Merton was engaged in his own experiment with truth—the truth of confronting what he termed the "Unspeakable." In his *Raids on the Unspeakable*, Merton wrote: "One of the awful facts of our age is the evidence that [the world] is stricken indeed, stricken to the very core of its being by the presence of the Unspeakable."[2]

In words that brought to mind the government's recently issued *Warren Report*, Merton described the Unspeakable:

> It is the void that contradicts everything that is spoken even before the words are said; the void that gets into the language of public and official declarations at the very moment when they are pronounced, and makes them ring dead with the hollowness of the abyss. It is the void out of which Eichmann drew the punctilious exactitude of his obedience.[3]

While corresponding with Merton, I also visited him periodically at his Gethsemani hermitage in 1965, a year in which

I taught theology at Bellarmine College in nearby Louisville. Those were illuminating times with Merton, but after his death he reached me more deeply with his writings. He died in Bangkok in 1968, apparently electrocuted by a faulty fan, only six months after Robert Kennedy was murdered in Los Angeles. Three decades later, at the end of the twentieth century, Merton's meditation on the Unspeakable became my lantern into the systemic darkness he had seen so profoundly in the institutions of Cold War America.

Looking back through Merton's eyes, I saw the Unspeakable as the void in which two revolutionary prophets, a president, and a president-to-be were all cut down. They were ambushed by what smelled like systemic evil, so entrenched in all four crime scenes that passive police forces caught no one except hapless scapegoats. Many Dealey Plaza witnesses to JFK's murder saw and heard what they thought was gunfire from the Grassy Knoll.[4] Yet attempting to identify the actual shooters, in the face of government denial and disinformation, meant running like a rat through a maze of traps. We were left, as Merton said, "frozen stiff before the face of the Unspeakable."[5] Yet, he added, that was precisely where Christian hope began, though "you will not find too many agreeing with you, even among Christians."[6]

I probed JFK's story first. My spiritual guide was the spirit of Merton, but the process was Gandhi's—an experiment with truth. What that meant was to research as relentlessly as possible, without reservations or a preconceived end, the truth of JFK's journey into the Unspeakable.

I discovered the dark hope Merton spoke of in the genesis of the hatred behind the president's murder. It came from the October 1962 confrontation between the United States and the Soviet Union over Soviet missiles in Cuba that brought the world to the brink of a nuclear war. In my research, I kept being struck by hope, even while "frozen stiff before the face of the Unspeakable," as the Pentagon clock almost struck midnight in the most terrible hours of the crisis. Kennedy's Joint Chiefs of Staff pressured him to order a surprise attack on the Soviet missile sites, leading toward an all-out nuclear war.[7] JFK resisted them. He

turned instead to his Cold War enemy, Soviet premier Nikita
Khrushchev. He sought Khrushchev's help to avert what threatened to become, in the president's words, "the final failure."[8] His
turn to Khrushchev, seen by some as treason, put him on the road
to Dallas.

By studying Kennedy's and Khrushchev's communications at
the edge of that abyss four decades later, I could see what was
truly an eleventh-hour hope. Jesus' blunt statement of reality,
"Love your enemies," was coming true in events that led finally
to the world's survival and the beginning transformation of two
apocalyptic warriors into peacemakers.[9] In horror and in hope,
Kennedy and Khrushchev did what Jesus said they (and we) must
do, for the sake of world peace—and a more daunting reward
for themselves (and ourselves). JFK would be killed because in
his final year he would keep on turning toward peace, regardless of the consequences to himself. He was following an ancient
law. Whether in response to Roman or Russian enemies, we had
to love those enemies—for the sake of everyone—in a truthful,
unsentimental way. Jesus' Hindu disciple, Gandhi, would identify that transforming *dharma* as *satyagraha* (truth-force or
soul-force). It was, in Merton's vision, the way to confront the
Unspeakable.

In probing our encounter with the Unspeakable, Merton was
not talking nonsense. He was drawing on the perennial wisdom
of contemplatives, prophets, and martyrs who faced evil without
flinching. Merton was uncovering for us a well into eternity from
whose living water we could all draw in the face of the Unspeakable in Dallas—and in Harlem, Memphis, and Los Angeles. To
enter those deep-water encounters with the Unspeakable is to see
in the murky shadows a light. It is where real hope begins.

Thomas Merton was rediscovering that hope in Gandhi.
While Merton was writing *Raids on the Unspeakable*, he was
also editing the writings of Gandhi for a book titled *Gandhi on
Non-Violence*.[10] Merton was confronting the Unspeakable out
of Gandhian nonviolence, drawn in turn, Merton emphasized,
from "a *universally valid* spiritual tradition which [Gandhi] saw
to be common to both East and West."[11]

In his essay, "A Tribute to Gandhi," Merton was impassioned in his identification of *satyagraha*, "truth-force," at the foundation of our very being: "Gandhi's religio-political action was based on an ancient metaphysic of humanity, a philosophical wisdom which is common to Hinduism, Buddhism, Islam, Judaism, and Christianity: that 'truth is the inner law of our being.'"[12]

As Merton in quoting Gandhi underlined, the other side of truth is love, whose living law is embodied in Jesus' death and teaching: "'Jesus died in vain,' said Gandhi, 'if he did not teach us to regulate the whole of life by the eternal law of love.'"[13]

Gandhi's nonviolence therefore required, Merton knew, "a supernatural courage only obtainable by prayer and spiritual discipline. This courage demands nothing short of the ability to face death with complete fearlessness and to suffer without retaliation."[14] Gandhi's courage in the face of death, the fruit of prayer and spiritual discipline, liberated him. He was free to live and proclaim a universal message of nonviolence. Gandhi's breakthrough "represented *the awakening of a new world*" (Merton's emphasis).[15] In the nuclear age, it came right on time. If we awaken to truth and nonviolence in the depths of a new world, we can confront the Unspeakable with hope.

The Unspeakable is not unique to the United States, nor to the assassinations of the '60s. We discover it in a less hidden way in Gandhi's murder. It exists in the shadow of all government and corporate power, but reaches a special depth of murderous deceit in a democracy with nuclear weapons. The Unspeakable that one finds in the assassinations of the '60s is the phenomenon of unaccountable power in a democracy killing, then lying about killing, with enough transparency for us to see we had better not go there. We are left with a void in our government's words and in our own, in even the thought of words. A terrible murder can occur amidst a void of responsibility.

In researching the murder of Gandhi, one encounters the Unspeakable in a newly independent India's struggle toward democracy combined with aspirations to greater power. Gandhi, like JFK, was killed by a conspiracy that threatened to destroy a democracy. The ominous dynamics underlying Gandhi's assassination were then effectively covered up—as would be true of the analogous murders in America. I began investigating Gandhi's death for an introductory chapter as background to the King and Malcolm stories. But the growing story of Gandhi's assassination, foreshadowing those of the American prophets, eventually became Gandhi's own book.

Mohandas Gandhi, soon after helping give birth to his country's independence, was killed by forces determined to destroy both him and his vision of a nonviolent, democratic India. Yet Gandhi walked hopefully into that conspiracy against hope. Gandhi, like Martin, Malcolm, and the Kennedys, foresaw his violent death. He prepared for the conclusion to his life for half a century. His increasing readiness to meet his assassin with love is the key to his encounter with the Unspeakable. As he became the prophet of the world's salvation by nonviolence, Gandhi trained himself, step by step, to die nonviolently to violence. It would be his final experiment with truth.

So let the reader be forewarned that this book celebrates dying, in the specific way Gandhi prepared to die, from the roots of his journey on the path of nonviolence and throughout his life. Walking with Gandhi means walking joyfully and nonviolently into God's arms—the arms of truth and love—through death. That is a way of hope. Because he prayed and prepared himself to die with love, Gandhi could meet his assassins' destructive conspiracy with hope.

What one also learns from Gandhi's murder, and from his assassins' trial, is that the story of Gandhi's assassination is not yet over. In the trial, the defendants tried to murder him all over again, this time by the assassination of both his character and his vision for the world. That process has continued for six decades. The successors to the organizations that nurtured Gandhi's assassins have kept on disseminating propaganda against him and his vision, while glossing over the assassination.[16] In the twenty-first century, they remain a threat to India's democracy. Their continued power is a measure of their success in repressing the truth of Gandhi's life and martyrdom.

Yet the story of Gandhi's assassination is a foundation for Merton's paradoxical hope, arising from those deadly encounters when we are "frozen stiff before the face of the Unspeakable." Gandhi was murdered in 1948 by the same kind of killing, lying power that was already working beneath the surface of the United States government as the Cold War began. Killing with "plausible deniability,"[17] as achieved in India by the architect of Gandhi's assassination, was already on the rise in the United States. Gandhi's murder, followed by the repression of its truth, forms a paradigm of killing and deceitful cover-up that U.S. citizens would soon have to confront in our own government. However, if we maintain the force of truth in the face of the Unspeakable, the darkness connecting Gandhi's murder with those of U.S. leaders can be overcome by light.

The politics of assassination has placed democracies on trial on opposite sides of the world. The Unspeakable remains in our midst. If we have the courage to confront it with the force of truth and love, as Gandhi did, hope prevails.

Jim Douglass
August 16, 2011

Seeds of Life and Death

Mohandas Karamchand Gandhi, known as "Mahatma" ("Great Soul"), was assassinated on January 30, 1948, two and a half years after the first use of weapons that could destroy all of humanity. Gandhi saw nuclear weapons as a confirmation of humanity's need to choose nonviolence for the sake of life itself. "I did not move a muscle," he said, "when I first heard that the atom bomb had wiped out Hiroshima. On the contrary, I said to myself, 'Unless now the world adopts nonviolence, it will spell certain suicide for humanity.' Nonviolence is the only thing the atom bomb cannot destroy."[1]

As Gandhi proclaimed his redemptive vision of a united, nonviolent India in the nuclear age, he was murdered by an anti-Muslim, Hindu nationalist group, with the silent complicity of forces in the newborn Indian government. A murderous nationalism, ambition for power, and hatred combined in Gandhi's assassination. India's achievement of independence made Gandhi's murder more feasible. The nation's new leaders had replaced its founding father's nonviolent principles with the foundations of a national security state. In the lengthening shadows of independence, Gandhi was a martyr to the unspeakable.[2]

Mohandas Gandhi began learning how to die in South Africa in the 1890s, through the perils of the first movement he organized. As he deepened in his understanding of dying, he wrote: "Just as one must learn the art of killing in the training

1

for violence, so one must learn the art of dying in the training for nonviolence."[3]

He had come from India to the British colony of Natal in South Africa as a twenty-three-year-old lawyer in May 1893. Soon after his arrival, he was thrown off a train because a white passenger objected to the "colored man's" presence in the same compartment. After struggling with his conscience all night in a freezing station, Gandhi decided to confront the systemic evil he had seen in action.[4] He became transformed from a shy, inarticulate lawyer into a determined organizer of his people against a system of laws that degraded them. In the course of three years, using the tactics of "polite constitutional protest,"[5] the Natal Indian Congress that Gandhi helped create was becoming a force for change in South Africa.

In January 1897, a South African mob tried to lynch Gandhi, on his return to the port of Durban in Natal. He was traveling with his wife, two sons, and a nephew after a six-month trip to India.

Gandhi's effort to educate the public in India about the discrimination against Indians in South Africa had placed his life in danger. A pamphlet he wrote and distributed widely in India was summarized in a distorted and exaggerated way in Natal's newspapers, outraging white South Africans. The papers also reported that Gandhi's incoming ship, the *Courland*, and an accompanying ship, the *Naderi*, had a total of more than five hundred Indians aboard, presumably to carry out a Gandhian plot to flood the white population with Indian immigrants. Mass meetings against an imminent Indian "invasion" were held in Natal, resulting in the formation of the "European Protection Society" and the "Colonial Patriotic Union." The groups combined to form a Demonstration Committee, whose avowed purpose was to prevent the Indians from landing at any cost.

Once the ships anchored in the outer reach of Durban's harbor on December 18, 1896, the government forced the passengers to wait on board. Attorney General Harry Escombe was Natal's acting prime minister at the time, due to the prime minister's

sick leave. Escombe indulged anti-Indian organizers by impos-
ing a twenty-three-day quarantine on the ships, under the bogus
danger of plague. The acting prime minister's purpose was
"to harass the passengers so that they might return to India."[6]
Europeans on shore became fanatically committed to the Indians' forced return to another continent, ignoring the fact that
the great majority were already legal residents in the process of
returning to their homes in South Africa.

Escombe was reported to have told the members of the
Demonstration Committee that "the government was 'wholly
with them'" and that "troops would not be called out even
if the demonstrators proceeded to take the law in their own
hands."[7] Attorney General Escombe had handed over the fate
of the Indian passengers to mob rule, with an eye toward winning the next election (when with the Demonstration Committee's support he would briefly become prime minister). With
Escombe's reassurances in their pocket, the members of the
Demonstration Committee were happy to take charge of the
situation. They spoke openly of throwing in the sea any Indians who had the gall to disembark. There was to be "no landing
at any price,"[8] especially for the demonstrators' prime target:
Mohandas Gandhi.

The quarantined passengers endured three cold, wet weeks,
under the threat of being lynched if they tried to set foot on
shore. Gandhi went about cheering them up, strengthening their
resolve to land. When the captain of the *Courland* held a Christmas dinner in honor of Gandhi and his family, he asked Gandhi
to speak to the assembled group. Gandhi told the Indian passengers that the origin of their present plight was Western civilization. He said, unlike the Eastern, it was based predominantly on
force.

The captain challenged him, saying, "Supposing the whites
carry out their threats, how will you stand by your principle of
nonviolence?"

Gandhi said, "I hope God will give me the courage and the
sense to forgive them and to refrain from bringing them to law. I
have no anger against them. I am only sorry for their ignorance

and their narrowness. I know that they sincerely believe that what they are doing today is right and proper. I have no reason therefore to be angry with them."

The captain smiled, "possibly distrustfully," as Gandhi recalled in his autobiography.[9]

When the quarantine was finally lifted, the Indian passengers prepared to disembark from the two ships. On that afternoon, January 13, 1897, Attorney General Escombe realized his folly and tried to counter the imminent threat of the massacre he had helped create. He spoke desperately, and as it turned out, persuasively to a mass meeting of the demonstrators. By promising his audience that the legislature would respond to their angry demands by restricting future Indian immigration, Escombe succeeded in dispersing most of the group. All the Indian passengers then managed to land safely with the exception of one man: Gandhi.[10]

Escombe had sent a message to Gandhi on the *Courland*, warning him not to leave the ship personally until evening, when the Superintendent of Water Police would escort him home. Gandhi, however, agreed with a friend who met him, Mr. Laughton, that he should not enter the city secretly, "like a thief in the night."[11] He disembarked openly and fearlessly in late afternoon under an overcast sky. With Laughton he began a perilous two-mile walk through Durban to a friend's home where his family was waiting for him. He was immediately identified as the notorious Gandhi.

A crowd gathered quickly. It surrounded the two men and began to stone Gandhi. An alarmed Laughton tried to hail a rickshaw to save Gandhi, but its puller, threatened by the crowd, ran for his life. Gandhi, who thought it "thoroughly disgusting to sit in a vehicle pulled by human beings,"[12] thanked God for saving him from the shame of that evil, although not having such a way out almost cost him his life.

The growing horde separated Gandhi from Laughton, pelted Gandhi with stones, and began beating and kicking him. Gandhi fainted but revived and clutched at the iron railings of a house. He held on as the beating intensified. He almost gave up hope of reaching home alive.

"But," he wrote later, "I remember well that even then my heart did not arraign my assailants."[13] His life was saved by the providential arrival of Mrs. Jane Alexander, the wife of Durban's police superintendent. As Mrs. Alexander tried to shield Gandhi with an umbrella, the police were alerted. A ring of officers formed around Gandhi. The protective cordon pushed slowly through the taunting throng of demonstrators to Gandhi's destination.

As darkness fell, a howling mob of five thousand people surrounded the house, determined to lynch Gandhi. "We'll burn him!" they screamed, threatening to torch the house and all its occupants unless they surrendered Gandhi.[14]

Police Superintendent Richard C. Alexander sent a detective into the house with an urgent message for Gandhi. If, the chief said, Gandhi wanted to save his friend, his friend's house, and his own family from the lynch mob, he should disguise himself as an Indian police officer and slip out. Gandhi followed Alexander's advice at once and, with two detectives also in disguise, escaped to the police station, where he remained for three days.

Jane and Richard Alexander saved Gandhi's life from enraged mobs that day through heroism and ingenuity. Yet ten months earlier, Police Superintendent Alexander had displayed what Gandhi biographer Narayan Desai described as "a general disregard and contempt for Indians," believing "that most Indians were violent coolies."[15] Alexander had tried to justify publicly a policeman's rough, arbitrary arrest of two Indian boys. Gandhi responded by publishing an open letter to the newly appointed police chief, appealing to his sense of justice behind his remark to a reporter that cases of "real grievance" would readily command his sympathy. Gandhi continued to express faith in the good will of Superintendent Alexander, who soon "became his staunch supporter and a friend of the Indian community"[16]—to the point where he and his wife, Jane, risked their lives to deliver Gandhi, his family, and friends from death.

When word of the mob violence in Natal reached London, the disturbed British authorities wired Attorney General Escombe, ordering him to prosecute Gandhi's assailants. Escombe found himself caught between the competing pressures of the British Empire's rulers, not wanting to jeopardize their control over the Indian subcontinent whose people Gandhi was representing in another context, and the empire's colonizers in South Africa, who wanted Gandhi's head without counting the cost. The besieged attorney general sent for Gandhi and asked him if he could identify any of his attackers.

Gandhi said, "I might perhaps be able to identify one or two of them. But I must say at once before this conversation proceeds that I have already made up my mind not to prosecute my assailants. I cannot see that they are at fault. What information they had, they had obtained from their leaders."

"If anyone is to blame," Gandhi pointed out, "it is the Committee of Europeans, you yourself, and therefore the Government of Natal. Now I cannot prosecute you or the Committee for the assault. And even if I could, I would not seek redress in a court of law. You took such steps as seemed advisable to you for safeguarding the interests of the Europeans of Natal. That is a political matter, and it remains for me to fight with you in the political field and to convince you and the other Europeans that the Indians who constitute a large proportion of the population of the British Empire wish to preserve their self-respect and safeguard their rights without injuring the Europeans in the least."[17]

Escombe saw his opponent was confronting him with uncomfortable truths, while at the same time restraining political furies that the attorney general had himself set loose. He said, "If you waive the right of bringing your assailants to book, you will considerably help me in restoring quiet, besides enhancing your own reputation."[18]

Gandhi took a blank piece of paper, wrote that he chose not to prosecute his attackers, signed it, and handed it to Escombe.

In his book, *Satyagraha in South Africa*, Gandhi thanked God for the entire life-threatening episode: "I had a most valuable experience, and whenever I think of that day, I feel that God was preparing me for the practice of Satyagraha."[19]

Harry Escombe and Mohandas Gandhi lived in the same neighborhood in Durban. Almost three years after the near-lynching, Escombe made a point of crossing the street one day to speak to the man walking on the other side, Gandhi.

He said, "Mr. Gandhi, I have long wished to tell you something that has lain on my mind. I am extremely sorry for what happened to you during the demonstration on your landing in Durban." Escombe expressed admiration for what he saw as the Indians' depth of Christian charity. He apologized for the anti-Asiatic laws he had passed—before, he said, he came to know the Indian community.[20]

Gandhi laughed, reassuring Escombe that, so far as he was concerned, their conflicts had been left in the past as soon as they occurred. He hoped with his neighbor there would be plenty of opportunity for them to work together in the future.

Three hours later, one of Escombe's servants came running to tell Gandhi in his home that Harry Escombe had just died of a heart attack.

When Gandhi spoke at a Durban ceremony years later to dedicate a statue of Harry Escombe, he revealed the final words his neighbor had spoken to him. Gandhi told the South African crowd honoring Escombe, "I want to do justice to the fairness and the magnanimity of the great man."[21]

Gandhi was learning step by step the art of dying in his training for nonviolence, but he had still not discovered *satyagraha*. He broke through to that transforming force of truth in the midst of his community's making a commitment to die for the truth.

On September 11, 1906, three thousand Indians packed the old Jewish Imperial Theater in Johannesburg, South Africa. The South African Indian community had come together to respond to a pending ordinance requiring that they carry registration cards, a critical degrading step toward their expulsion from the country. Gandhi had helped draft a resolution that the Indians would not submit to the law and would instead suffer the penalties for their refusal.

When the resolution was proposed and seconded, an old, experienced Muslim leader, Sheth Haji Habib, passionately declared to the mass meeting that, "in the name of God," he would never submit to the law. He appealed to everyone present to join him in taking such an oath before God.

In describing this moment, Gandhi says, "I was taken aback by Sheth Haji Habib's suggestion of an oath. I thought out the possible consequences of it in a moment. My perplexity gave place to enthusiasm. And although I had no intention of taking an oath or inviting others to do so when I went to the meeting, I warmly approved of the Sheth's suggestion."[22]

Gandhi rose to speak to the crowd about the crucial implications of adding Sheth Haji Habib's oath to the resolution. He said:

> I wish to explain to this meeting that there is a vast difference between this resolution and every other resolution we have passed up to date and that there is a wide divergence also in the manner of making it. It is a very grave resolution we are making, as our existence in South Africa depends upon our fully observing it.
>
> We all believe in one and the same God, the differences of nomenclature in Hinduism and Islam notwithstanding. To pledge ourselves or to take an oath in the name of that God or with him as witness is not something to be trifled with. If having taken such an oath we violate our pledge we are guilty before God and man.
>
> This pledge must not be taken with a view to produce an effect on outsiders. No one should trouble to consider what impression it might have upon the Local Government, the Imperial Government, or the Government of India. Everyone must only search his own heart, and if the inner voice assures him that he has the requisite strength to carry him

through, then only should he pledge himself and then only will his pledge bear fruit.

A few words now as to the consequences.... We may have to go to jail, where we may be insulted. We may have to go hungry and suffer extreme heat or cold. Hard labor may be imposed upon us. We may be flogged by rude warders. We may be fined heavily and our property may be attached and held up to auction if there are only a few resisters left. Opulent today we may be reduced to abject poverty tomorrow. We may be deported. Suffering from starvation and similar hardships in jail, some of us may fall ill and even die.... But I can boldly declare, and with certainty, that so long as there is even a handful of men true to their pledge, there can only be one end to the struggle, and that is victory.

It is possible that a majority of those present here may take the pledge in a fit of enthusiasm or indignation but may weaken under the ordeal, and only a handful may be left to face the final test. Even then there is only one course open to someone like me, to die but not to submit to the law.... Everyone should fully realize his responsibility, then only pledge himself independently of others and understand that he himself must be true to his pledge even unto death, no matter what others do.[23]

Gandhi sat down. The crowd had listened to him in silence, absorbing his explanation of the nature of the commitment that now lay before them. Finally, three thousand people stood. With upraised hands, they took an oath: With God as their witness, they would not submit to the law.

Although no one knew what to call it, a new kind of movement had just been born. In January 1908, Gandhi offered a small prize in his journal, *Indian Opinion*, to the reader who could come up with "the best designation for our struggle." Gandhi liked the suggestion "sadagraha," meaning "firmness in a good cause," but felt it "did not fully represent the whole idea

I wished it to connote. I therefore corrected it to 'Satyagraha.' Truth (*Satya*) implies love, and firmness (*agraha*) engenders and therefore serves as a synonym for force. I thus began to call the Indian movement 'Satyagraha,' that is to say, the Force which is born of Truth and Love or nonviolence."[24]

The oath taken by the Indian people at the Imperial Theater marked the beginning of the *satyagraha* movement in South Africa and India, the beginning of the end of imperial rule. For those who joined in what Gandhi would later identify by the term *satyagraha,* their struggle would include all of the suffering yet liberating consequences Gandhi understood as the fruits of such a commitment. The transforming power of *satyagraha* was born through his people's solemn oath of nonviolent resistance to the point of death taken on September 11, 1906.

The spiritual roots of *satyagraha* lay even more deeply in Gandhi's own personal vows of nonviolence, which he had taken recently, celibacy, the renunciation of wealth, and the service of humanity, especially the poor. It was Gandhi's own path of self-renunciation and service that gave him the profound freedom to call for a nonviolent commitment of their very lives from his people that would change India and the world. Purify the source, he was discovering, and anything was possible.

In Gandhi's next close encounter with a violent death, also in South Africa, he took the way he hoped to respond to an attack one step further—to expire with the name of God on his lips. This time he was assaulted not by a government-instigated mob but by an Indian co-worker in the *satyagraha* movement. His ally thought Gandhi had become a traitor to their cause.

In 1907, when the British colony of the Transvaal became independent, its government passed the Transvaal Asiatic Registration Act (TARA), an extension of the legislation the Indian community had taken an oath to resist. The law required all Asiatics to register with the government, be fingerprinted like criminals, and carry their registration cards at all times. Gandhi told the Transvaal interior minister, General Jan Christian Smuts, Indians would in conscience have to resist TARA, which was aimed at them. When the vast majority of 13,000 Indians living in the Transvaal then refused to register, Gandhi was one of the first charged. He was sentenced to two months in prison—his first jail term.[25]

Two weeks later, General Smuts sent a proposal for a compromise to Gandhi in his Johannesburg jail cell. The police superintendent of Johannesburg took Gandhi in his prison uniform to the interior minister's office in Pretoria. Smuts, aware that thousands of Indians were prepared to follow Gandhi to jail, wanted to negotiate. He promised Gandhi that if the majority of the Indians underwent voluntary registration, the government would then repeal the law and consider the matter closed. Gandhi, believing strongly he should trust his opponent, agreed to Smuts's proposal.

Smuts said, "I do not wish there should be any recurrence of the trouble, and I wish to respect the feelings of your people."[26] He then freed Gandhi, who borrowed his train fare home from Smuts's secretary.

On his arrival in Johannesburg at 9:00 that night, Gandhi called a public meeting for midnight to present the results of his negotiation with Smuts. The friends he spoke with in advance were skeptical of the settlement, saying: What if Smuts broke faith with them? By registering voluntarily, they would surrender in advance the most powerful weapon they had for resisting TARA. The right order for the settlement, they argued, was to get TARA repealed before making any such concession.[27]

Gandhi acknowledged the force of their argument. Yet he thought a satyagrahi (a practitioner of truth-force) needed to place full trust in the opponent. Smuts's promise had provided them with a teaching moment in the path of nonviolence, but it was a very hard teaching.

He said, "A satyagrahi bids goodbye to fear. He is therefore never afraid of trusting the opponent. Even if the opponent plays him false twenty times, the satyagrahi is ready to trust him for the twenty-first time, for an implicit trust in human nature is the very essence of his creed."

At the same time, trusting the government did not mean giving up the power of noncooperation. "Suppose we register voluntarily," he said, "but the government commits a breach of faith and fails to redeem its promise to repeal the Act. Could we not then resort to satyagraha? If we refused to show at the proper time the certificates of registration we take out, our registration would count for nothing, and government could not distinguish between ourselves and the Indians who might enter the Transvaal surreptitiously. Therefore, whether there is or there is not any law in force, the government cannot exercise control over us without our cooperation.... We are fearless and free, so long as we have the weapon of satyagraha in our hands."[28]

Gandhi managed to dispel the doubts of his skeptical friends, but as he wrote later, "I did not then even dream of the storm which was to break out at the midnight meeting."[29]

Word spread quickly among the Indians in Johannesburg about their leader's questionable compromise with Smuts. A thousand people gathered on the grounds of a mosque at midnight to hear what he had to say.

Speaking in the glow of hurricane lamps, Gandhi explained to his listeners why it was right to do now what they had vowed with him never to do—register under a notorious law. He said a compromise called for both parties to make concessions where a principle was not at stake. Smuts, by promising to repeal the law, was withdrawing government coercion from the act of registration. The stigma had been removed from a law that, as promised, would soon be repealed. It would never be enforced. In return, as an act of good faith, the Indians should register voluntarily, conceding thereby the government's right to prevent illegal immigration.

Gandhi appealed to the Indians to go out and organize the community in an opposite direction, moving from noncooperation to trust and cooperation with their opponents.

"Just as many of you had volunteered before in order to explain to our compatriots why they should not register, even so should you now come forward to explain to the community why they must register. And it is only when we have thus worthily fulfilled our part that we shall reap the real fruit of our victory."[30]

When Gandhi concluded, a Pathan friend and client of his, Mir Alam, objected to his new position. Alam asked angrily why it was all right now for Indians to give their fingerprints to the government. They were still being treated as criminals.

Gandhi said the difference came from changed circumstances:

I say with all the force at my command, that what would have been a crime against the people yesterday is in the altered circumstances of today the hallmark of a gentleman. If you require me to salute you by force and if I submit to you, I will have demeaned myself in the eyes of the public and in your eyes as well as in my own. But if I of my own accord salute you as a brother or fellow man, that evinces my humility and gentlemanliness.[31]

Mir Alam was unconvinced.

"We have heard," he said, "that you have betrayed the community and sold it to General Smuts for 15,000 pounds. We will never give the fingerprints nor allow others to do so. I swear with Allah as my witness that I will kill the man who takes the lead in applying for registration."[32]

Gandhi said,

I will render all possible help to any Pathan or other who wishes to register without giving fingerprints, and I assure him that he will get the certificate all right without violence being done to his conscience. I must confess, however, that I do not like the threat of death that the friend has held out....

Whether or not he carries out his threat, as the principal party responsible for this settlement and as a servant of the community, it is my clear duty to take the lead in giving fingerprints, and I pray to God that He graciously permit me to do so. Death is the appointed end of all life. To die by the hand of a brother, rather than by disease or in such other way, cannot be for me a matter for sorrow.[33]

On February 10, 1908, Gandhi was prepared to take the lead in registering that morning. When he stopped by his law office, he found Mir Alam and several companions standing outside—not waiting in the office, as Alam had often done in the past when he sought Gandhi's advice. Alam offered no greeting. His eyes were full of anger. Gandhi thought something was going to happen.

When Gandhi and other Indian leaders set out for the registration office, Mir Alam and his companions followed. As Gandhi approached the government building, Alam stepped in front of him. He asked Gandhi where he was going.

"I propose to take out a certificate of registration giving the ten fingerprints," Gandhi answered. "If you will go with me, I will first get you a certificate, with an impression only of the two thumbs, and then I will take one for myself, giving the fingerprints."[34]

Gandhi was suddenly clubbed on the head. He fell down unconscious with the words, "He Rama!" (Oh God!) on his lips. Mir Alam and his companions kept clubbing and kicking the unconscious Gandhi. They also struck him with a lead pipe. Gandhi's friends tried to intervene and were also beaten. The assailants, thinking Gandhi dead, fled.[35]

As Mir Alam had sworn, the intent was to kill the first registrant, Gandhi. The attackers meant business. Thambi Naidoo, Gandhi's co-worker who tried to shield him, was beaten so badly on his head that he suffered dizzy spells the rest of his life.[36]

Where did Gandhi get his mantra, "Rama" (God), that he hoped would be on his lips when he died?

He tells us in his autobiography that as a child he was haunted by a fear of thieves, ghosts, and serpents. Because of his fear, he always had to sleep with a light in his room.

A loving nurse, Rambha, recommended to young Mohandas that, to overcome his fear, he should simply repeat God's name. Although he did not continue to practice the mantra as a child, he thought later that it was "due to the seed sown by that good woman Rambha that today *Ramanama* is an infallible remedy for me."[37]

The repetition of God's name in Gandhi's inner being became the heart of his spiritual practice. He said, "I am a stranger to yogic practices.... [The practice] I learned in my childhood has become a huge thing in my mental firmament. It is a sun that has brightened my darkest hour. A Christian may find the same solace from the repetition of the name of Jesus, and a Muslim from the name of Allah.... Only the repetition must not be a lip expression, but part of your very being."[38]

When shot to death in 1948, he would say as he fell, "Rama! Rama!"[39]

Gandhi regained consciousness from Mir Alam's assault in a nearby office. A friend bending over him was asking how he felt.

"I am all right," Gandhi said, "but there is pain in the teeth and the ribs. Where is Mir Alam?"

"He has been arrested along with the rest."

"They should be released."[40]

As friends treated Gandhi's wounds, he insisted on having registration papers brought to him at once so he could fulfill his pledge to register first. He then wired the attorney general not to prosecute Mir Alam and the others. (Because the assault was public and had other witnesses—Gandhi refused to testify—Alam and a second man were charged and served short sentences.)

Although stitches in Gandhi's cheeks and upper lip prevented speech, he was able to write a message to the Indian community. He emphasized his hope that the government would not prosecute Mir Alam: "[Mir Alam and company] had acted in the only way they knew against what they thought to be wrong. Hindus should not retain anger against Muslims."[41] From the very beginning of his public life in South Africa, Gandhi focused on Hindu-Muslim unity as a prerequisite for achieving Indians' freedom.

Mir Alam was true to his word and tried to kill Gandhi before he could register. General Smuts, on the other hand, did not fulfill his promise to repeal the registration act. Smuts not only continued the old law, he also got the legislature to enact a second anti-Asiatic law validating the registrations given in good faith by the Indians after the old law's deadline had passed.

Gandhi was astounded when he read the new bill. His skeptical critics now seemed right in regard to Smuts. Gandhi, commenting later on this sequence of events, continued to give Smuts the benefit of the doubt, saying it was possible he "was not guilty of a deliberate breach of faith."[42] Nevertheless, the government's further repression called for an upsurge of nonviolent resistance.

On Sunday, August 16, 1908, Gandhi's Satyagraha Association convened a meeting of three thousand Indians at the Hamidia Mosque in Johannesburg. They had come to celebrate a new stage of *satyagraha* by the burning of their registration certificates. An iron caldron with four legs stood on a platform. It was filled with two thousand certificates already handed in.

Gandhi spoke to the crowd, saying: "It is because I ask you to suffer everything that may be necessary [rather] than break your oath, it is because I expect this of my countrymen, that they will be, above all, true to their God, that I ask you this afternoon to burn all these certificates."[43]

The Satyagraha Association had informed the government that the certificates would not be burned if it would repeal TARA and "stop the passage of the Asiatic Act in its new and revised form."[44] At 4:00 p.m. a messenger on a bicycle delivered the government's telegraphed response. When it was announced that the authorities were still determined to pass the Act, the people cheered, knowing their imminent act of resistance was confirmed. More of them rushed forward, adding certificates to the caldron. As the bonfire was lit, the crowd roared in approval.

Mir Alam, having served his jail sentence, joined Gandhi on the platform. He said he "had done wrong in assaulting Gandhi," who then grasped his hand and said he bore no resentment toward his friend.[45]

Gandhi's friend, Millie Polak, the wife of his close co-worker Henry Polak, has shared another incident in 1908 in which Gandhi was confronted by an attacker.

At the end of a big organizing meeting of the Indian community in Johannesburg, Gandhi and Millie Polak walked out of a crowded hall. Polak noticed a man in the shadows by the door. Gandhi went to the man, linked arms with him, and said something quietly.

Years later, Polak described what happened next:

> The man hesitated for one moment, then turned and walked away with Mr. Gandhi, I meantime keeping my place on the other side of him. We walked the length of the street....Both men were speaking in a very low voice. At the end of the street the man handed something over to Mr. Gandhi and walked away....
>
> "What did the man want—anything special?" I queried.
>
> "Yes," replied Mr. Gandhi, "he wanted to kill me."
>
> "To kill you," I repeated. "To kill you? How horrible! Is he mad?"
>
> "No, he thinks that I am acting traitorously towards our people; that I am intriguing with the government against them, and yet pretending to be their friend and leader."
>
> "But that is all wicked and dreadful," I protested. "Such a man is not safe; he ought to be arrested. Why did you let him go like that? He must be mad!"
>
> "No," replied Mr. Gandhi, "he is not mad, only mistaken; and you saw, after I had talked to him, he handed over to me the knife he had intended to use on me."
>
> "He would have stabbed you in the dark. I...."
>
> But Mr. Gandhi interrupted me. "Do not disturb yourself so much about it. He thought he wanted to kill me; but he really had not the courage to do so. If I were as bad as he thought I was, I should deserve to die. Now we will not worry any more about it. It is finished. I do not think that man will attempt to injure me again. Had I had him

arrested I should have made an enemy of him. As it is, he will now be my friend."[46]

Between three and four thousand Indians went to jail in the Transvaal in 1908 and 1909 for their nonviolent resistance to the registration law.[47] In June 1910, as the Transvaal became part of the newly created Union of South Africa, Gandhi's Transvaal adversary, General Jan Christian Smuts, became South Africa's interior minister. Smuts now negotiated with Gandhi on behalf of the national government.

On March 14, 1913, the Cape division of the Supreme Court gave a judgment that outraged the Indian women of South Africa. Justice Malcolm Searle ruled that the wives of non-Christian marriages had no right to immigrate to South Africa. Gandhi pointed out quickly in his journal, *Indian Opinion*, that, as a result of the court's ruling, all "Hindu or Muslim wives living in South Africa lose their right to live there ... [and] it is quite on the cards that the government will not permit any more wives to come in."[48]

Gandhi took the court's judgment as God's invitation to a deepening, widening *satyagraha*. It gave him the opportunity to mobilize "the committed core of the satyagraha movement."[49] In the process, his wife, Kasturba, decided to join other Indian women at Gandhi's Phoenix Ashram in courting arrest by crossing the border between Natal and the Transvaal without permits. In September, Kasturba was arrested with fifteen companions, including the Gandhis' fifteen-year-old son, Ramdas, and was sentenced to three months in prison with hard labor.[50]

When Kasturba's group went to prison, Gandhi was elated. He sensed a leaven in the Indian community was about to produce a profound change in the South African body politic. He was right. A second group of women, from Gandhi's Tolstoy Farm, were inspired by their incarcerated sisters. As Gandhi wrote in *Indian Opinion*, "They were fired with the desire to be in jail."[51] Mothers with children in their arms led their families out of Tolstoy Farm, on their own walk to freedom. They went to the coal mines at Newcastle, where they proclaimed a non-violent revolution to thousands of indentured Indian miners.

Gandhi could hardly believe what was happening, after years of planting seeds of nonviolence in the ashram families:

> The mere presence of these women [among the coal miners] was like a lighted matchstick to dry fuel. Women who had never before slept except on soft beds and had seldom so much as opened their mouths, now delivered public speeches among the indentured laborers. The latter were roused and, even before I arrived, were all for commencing the strike. The project was full of risk…. By the time I reached there, Indians in two coal mines had already stopped work.[52]

In October 1913, between four and five thousand indentured Indian coal miners in northern Natal joined the *satyagraha* movement by going on strike. Following Gandhi's recommendation, they vowed not to return to work until the government repealed its repressive three-pound tax on all ex-indentured workers. Gandhi's call to resist the three-pound tax touched a revolutionary nerve in the indentured workers. The effect of the three-pound tax with a depressed economy had been to remove "the time limit from indentured labor. Workers forced back under contract by tax debts and unemployment (and, indeed, those who had yet to complete their first period of indenture) faced, for all they knew, a lifetime on the plantations or [in] the mines."[53]

When the coal miners walked off their jobs, they and their families remained critically dependent on the mine owners for food and shelter. The owners asked to meet with Gandhi. He told them that the strikers "would be immediately advised to resume work, regardless of any other grievances,"[54] as soon as the government committed itself to repeal the three-pound tax. The coal owners, forced by negotiator Gandhi to choose between supporting the government or the strikers, did not hesitate. They ordered that rations be withheld from the miners until they returned to work. To add to the coercion, the owners shut off the electricity in the miners' homes.

Confronted by the owners' ultimatum, Gandhi and a growing wave of strikers departed from the mine compounds. They headed toward the border, where they anticipated being arrested for crossing illegally into the Transvaal. Gandhi, who now had the chore of feeding two thousand workers and their families every day, did not fear the prospect of a mass arrest that would shift the burden of sustenance from himself to the government.[55]

General Smuts took shrewd stock of the situation. He held off ordering an arrest when the marchers entered the Transvaal. Smuts observed confidently: "Mr. Gandhi appeared to be in a position of much difficulty. Like Frankenstein he found his monster an uncomfortable creation and he would be glad to be relieved of further responsibility for its support."[56]

Over two thousand striking miners and 150 women and children were now committed to an exhausting march, which Gandhi projected for eight days to his community at Tolstoy Farm. Each day an emergency support system, made up principally of a sympathetic European baker and supportive European railway officials, rushed a ration of bread and sugar to the long column of advancing strikers.[57] Covering twenty to twenty-four miles a day, the marchers had to endure hunger, fatigue, the elements, and the threats of local European residents. Some died in transit. But the rebellious march continued into the Transvaal.

Smuts felt compelled to do something. He tried to stop the nonviolent invasion by plucking Gandhi from it.

Gandhi was arrested on the first and third days. He was bailed out twice so as to continue leading the march. On the fourth day, he was arrested again, tried quickly, and with the help of his own testimony, convicted and sentenced to nine months at hard labor in a remote prison.

As Gandhi had urged, in his absence the strikers kept on marching toward Tolstoy Farm. What seemed like a daily miracle of loaves and sugar continued to happen. Smuts realized his waiting game in regard to a mass arrest had failed. Allowing the march to go forward was proving counterproductive. The strikers' courage was spreading to the country's other indentured workers, who began walking off one plantation after another.

On the fifth day, all two thousand marchers were arrested. Many had walked 110 miles by then.[58] The police herded the strikers onto trains that took them back to their mine compounds. Guards imprisoned the miners by wire nets placed over their mines. They were ordered to resume work. The miners refused and were whipped. They kept on refusing at the cost of more whippings.

The miners' resistance inspired tens of thousands of other Indian workers to go out on strike. The police tried desperately to force the Indians back to work—charging them on horses, shooting and killing several, and injuring many more by beatings. As reports of the widening *satyagraha* struggle went around the world, international support rallied behind the movement.

In December, the government released Gandhi unconditionally and approved a commission "to investigate the grievances of the Indians in South Africa."[59] Gandhi questioned the anti-Indian composition of the commission, which he felt was being set up to dupe public opinion. He refused to cooperate with it. Instead, he announced on January 1, 1914, that he and other Indians were about to begin a new march from Durban to court arrest. The Indian community was re-igniting massive civil resistance.

Then, as the South African government was paralyzed by a nationwide strike of European railroad workers, Gandhi suddenly reversed course, following his nonviolent logic. He said, "Satyagrahis would not take advantage of an opponent's accidental difficulties."[60] He cancelled the march. As his biographer Geoffrey Ashe commented, "The moral impact was overwhelming. Messages of congratulation poured in from England, India, even South Africa."[61]

A secretary to General Smuts described to Gandhi the moral dilemma the Indians' nonviolence had created:

I do not like your people, and do not care to assist them at all. But what am I to do? You help us in our days of need. How can we lay hands upon you? I often wish you took to violence like the English strikers, and then we would know at once how to dispose of you. But you will not injure even the enemy. You desire victory by self-suffering alone and never transgress your self-imposed limits of courtesy and chivalry. And that is what reduces us to sheer helplessness.[62]

Smuts had reached a similar conclusion. He no longer had the will to fight Gandhi. He negotiated a settlement with the Indians in the spring of 1914. The government cancelled the three-pound tax, recognized the rights of Indian wives, and repealed the remaining parts of the Transvaal Asiatic Registration Act that the movement had resisted. Over six thousand South African Indians had gone to prison in the nine-year-long *satyagraha* struggle.[63]

Gandhi's settlement with Smuts was again rejected by segments of the Indian community. They included Muslims who felt their "religious right of polygamy was compromised"[64] because the bill provided for only one lawful wife at a time. Co-workers warned Gandhi about the dangers of attending a March 1914 Muslim meeting in Johannesburg. Gandhi insisted on going.

At the volatile meeting, when he explained his settlement to the audience, Gandhi met bitter challenges. Accusations followed. An element in the crowd seemed ready to assault him. Then, as his biographer Narayan Desai narrates, "suddenly a tall, well-built and angry Pathan came forward, brandishing a naked dagger."[65] It was Mir Alam, the man who had beaten Gandhi into unconsciousness in 1908, almost killing him.

This time Mir Alam turned from Gandhi to the audience. He said, "Beware, there are some mischief-makers in the meeting ready to attack Gandhibhai. If anyone harms him, he will fall victim to my dagger."

Gandhi smiled at the man he had always regarded as his friend. He said, "Mir Alam! Why are you so angry? Come near me. We are all brothers. No one is going to attack me."

Mir Alam knew better. He cried out, "You are a fakir! You do not know, but I know everything. The man who steps forward to harm you will be finished at that very instant!"[66]

The crowd was silent. Gandhi stayed to the end of the meeting. Mir Alam accompanied Gandhi and his co-workers safely to their residence.

Gandhi's intended assassin for his compromise with Smuts in 1908 had become his protector against those endangering him for a similar grievance in 1914.

That summer Gandhi left South Africa for England and India and never returned.

In the course of the South African government's efforts to crush the Indian resistance, General Smuts, unlike Harry Escombe, was never linked to a life-threatening assault on Gandhi. Smuts did, however, command forces that shot and killed Indian resisters. He repeatedly jailed Gandhi and thousands of his co-workers, some of whom died from harsh prison conditions. The South African leader also deceived Gandhi and the *satyagraha* movement repeatedly by his words. He used virtually every political weapon at his disposal. Smuts sensed that Gandhi's militant nonviolence was momentous in terms of the stakes it raised for the country.

Smuts was right. As Nelson Mandela pointed out at the end of the twentieth century, Gandhi's *satyagraha* challenge to the South African government at the beginning of the century laid a foundation for the anti-apartheid movement. "The African People's Organization (APO) was established in 1902, the ANC in 1912," Mandela said, "so that both were witnesses to and highly influenced by Gandhi's militant satyagraha which began in 1907 and reached its climax in 1913 with the epic march."[67]

The Gandhi-Smuts struggle also tested Gandhi's nonviolent resolve to remain civil and loving toward his crafty, politically astute opponent, who stamped out opposition any way he could. Gandhi confessed, "When I was corresponding with him and writing in the paper against him, I remember I had taken General Smuts to be a heartless man." Yet Gandhi searched more deeply for grace in his opponent, without abandoning a sharply critical perspective: "From our subsequent talks I often felt that the general belief in South Africa about General Smuts's cunning did him perhaps less than justice. I am however sure of two things. First, he has some principles in politics, which are not quite immoral. Secondly, there is room in his politics for cunning and on occasions for perversion of truth."[68]

Smuts in turn was not unhappy to see Gandhi transfer his experiments with truth from South Africa to India in 1914. Smuts said with relief: "The saint has left our shores, I sincerely hope forever."[69]

When Smuts finally conceded victory to the *satyagraha* campaign, Gandhi on his departure from South Africa presented his wily adversary with the farewell gift of a pair of sandals he had made for him in jail. Smuts was moved by his prisoner's present. He took good care of the sandals over the years.

In a tribute to Gandhi published on his seventieth birthday, Smuts said, "I have worn these sandals for many a summer since [I received them from Gandhi], even though I may feel that I am not worthy to stand in the shoes of so great a man!"[70]

As Gandhi was leading India to independence in the 1940s, Smuts had become the prime minister of South Africa. Smuts then tried to warn the man who had become Gandhi's foremost opponent and current jailor, British Prime Minister Winston Churchill, that he didn't know the kind of power he was up against. Smuts did know. When he was with Churchill in Cairo in 1942, Smuts told him, "[Gandhi] is a man of God. You and I are mundane people. Gandhi has appealed to religious motives. You never have. That is where you have failed."[71]

But Churchill didn't get it. Or didn't want to. The British prime minister tried to make a joke in response to Smuts's suggestion that Gandhi was drawing on a higher power. Smuts just gazed at Churchill with a deeply serious expression.[72]

Smuts's characterization of Gandhi to Churchill was apt but incomplete. Gandhi's discovery of *satyagraha* did involve, as

Smuts said, a religious appeal. But it was not an appeal Winston Churchill could have made without becoming poor. Churchill would have first been compelled to live, as Gandhi did, in the same poverty his country's poorest citizens lived in. Gandhi's way to God was through suffering people. He immersed himself in the everyday details of their lives. There he discovered, through meditation and prayer, nonviolent ways to transform oppression into freedom.

In his experiments with truth, Gandhi was developing a deeper, broader kind of power than politicians knew. *Satyagraha* drew ultimately on the awakening power of the poorest, most enslaved Indians in South Africa, the indentured workers with whom Gandhi bonded in resistance to the three-pound tax. Gandhi's experiments would awaken that kind of slumbering power in hundreds of millions of poor people on his return to India. The power of the powerless would make him, who had no ambition for power, an increasing threat to those who did. The radical politics of *satyagraha* would begin to eclipse the established politics of dominance.

Yet the British Empire was resilient even in its decline. Its leaders would maintain a crumbling rule over India by dividing Muslims from Hindus in separate elections and representation, while Gandhi would work constantly for Hindu-Muslim unity, just as he had in South Africa. The imperial policy of divide and rule would be embraced eventually in India and the emerging state of Pakistan by both Hindu and Muslim politicians. Gandhi's only power in swimming against the divisive imperial tide, in India as in South Africa, was *satyagraha*—the nonviolent power of a unifying truth lived out by himself and many others, regardless of the cost to themselves.

Satyagraha was the revolutionary force of truth Gandhi discovered in his own life and in the lives of his people. If he and they were willing to come together, Hindus and Muslims alike, and give their lives for the truth, then bullets, bombs, and jails were powerless against them. General Smuts had seen enough of that force of truth in South Africa to know Winston Churchill was liable to be frustrated. Churchill could call on the might of the British Empire, but Gandhi could call on a force more powerful. Churchill was trying to stop a fearless force whose capacity to transform the world was, as Gandhi understood, nothing less than the power of God. Gandhi was determined to give his life totally to that power.

In retrospect one can see what Gandhi was getting into in his experiments with truth in South Africa. In his discovery of *satyagraha* lay the seeds of both Indian independence and his own assassination.

Gandhi and His Assassins

Gandhi knew his assassins.

He was reported to have encountered earlier the man who fired the gun that killed him. Gandhi was said to have invited the future triggerman to live with him for a week—after the man was arrested in an earlier, failed attempt to kill him.

Gandhi knew well the Hindu nationalist ideology of the conspirators plotting diligently to murder him. Their group was the fanatical core of a rising movement that would fracture India then and today threatens to dominate it.

Gandhi knew especially the spiritual leader behind his assassination, a brilliant Indian thinker on revolutionary violence whom he had met in London four decades before. The two men's developing visions of violence and nonviolence, terrorism and *satyagraha* (truth-force), assassination and martyrdom, competed then—and compete now with greater urgency—for the future of India and the world.

The intertwined stories of Gandhi and his assassins give us an interpretive lens with which to see reality. We live in a world where assassination has become an unspeakable, nationally approved art to frustrate fundamental change in proudly democratic countries, ranging from India to the United States of America.

In 1909, while he was discovering *satyagraha* in South Africa, Gandhi made the second of two frustrating trips to London to petition the imperial government on behalf of his besieged community. His 1909 lobbying, like his previous effort in 1906, reinforced for Gandhi the futility of addressing the center of power from a position of weakness. To speak from a position of strength, Gandhi needed to represent more of his people, the masses of whom lived in India, not South Africa. Gandhi was already feeling a deep need to return to India, where the independence movement was gaining strength.

In his 1909 trip, Gandhi also learned to his alarm how much a new generation of Indians was being drawn toward assassination and armed struggle as the only way for them to be liberated from the British. In fact the sensational news of an assassination, carried out proudly by an Indian nationalist, greeted him on his arrival in London on July 10, 1909.

On July 1, London was shocked when Sir William Curzon Wyllie, political aide to the secretary of state for India, was shot to death by an Indian student. The murder took place at a lavish reception held by the National Indian Association at the Institute of Imperial Studies in the heart of London. The assassin was Madanlal Dhingra, a recent engineering graduate from University College, London. When a Parsee doctor who was with Wyllie struggled with Dhingra, the assassin used his final shots to kill the doctor.

Wyllie and Dhingra knew each other. Wyllie was a friend of Madanlal Dhingra's family. Dhingra's father in India, a prominent doctor loyal to the British crown, had even appealed to his British friend, Wyllie, to guide Madanlal away from militant student activism in London.[1] In Wyllie's final moments, he may have realized how little chance there was of that. As Wyllie was about to leave the reception, Madanlal came up to him in a friendly way as if to say good night, hiding his pistol in his hands. He suddenly fired two shots into Wyllie's face, then two more into his body as it fell to the floor, killing him on the spot.[2]

Dhingra's motive was political. He had become a dedicated follower of Vinayak Damodar Savarkar, a twenty-six-year-old Indian philosopher of violent revolution and assassination. Savarkar was the leader of a cadre of militant Indian students living at a London hostel he ran, India House. He had molded

Madanlal Dhingra for months as an assassin. Savarkar assigned Dhingra the mission of killing Wyllie. It was Dhingra's second assignment. He had failed his prior mission from Savarkar to murder the secretary of state for India, when a door closed between the shooter and his target. Savarkar was furious. When Dhingra asked his mentor's blessing for his attempt to assassinate Wyllie, Savarkar just gave him a revolver and said, "If you fail this time, don't show me your face again."[3]

When Dhingra succeeded in killing Wyllie, who was known as "the eye and brain of India Office,"[4] Savarkar congratulated his jailed disciple on his achievement. He also used the condemned assassin as his shield and mouthpiece.

On August 18, the day after Dhingra's execution, Savarkar succeeded through friendly press contacts in getting the full text of "Dhingra's statement" published in the *London Daily News*. Dhingra is cited as saying: "I admit, the other day I attempted to shed English blood as an humble revenge for the inhuman hangings and deportations of patriotic Indian youths. In this attempt I have consulted none but my own conscience; I have conspired with none but my own duty."[5] These words, written by Savarkar,[6] defend the murder in the name of the man who pulled the trigger, while at the same time covering up the author of the conspiracy—Savarkar himself.[7]

Madanlal Dhingra was himself so committed to covering up the man who was sacrificing him to the British that he told other Savarkar followers, "If we live and Savarkar dies, all of us put together cannot make even one Savarkar, but if I die and Savarkar lives, he can make hundreds of Madanlals."[8]

Gandhi, having arrived in London nine days after Wyllie's murder, watched with growing concern the playing out of the assassination drama, climaxed by Dhingra's execution, which many Indian nationalists saw as the death of a hero. Gandhi had known Wyllie. He mourned his death. He could also feel sympathy for Dhingra, not as a hero but as a man overcome by a destructive idea. As always, Gandhi made his thoughts public. He said, "In my view, Mr. Dhingra himself is innocent. The murder was committed in a state of intoxication. It is not merely wine or *bhang* that makes one drunk; a mad idea can also do so. That was the case with Mr. Dhingra."[9]

Gandhi said he thought those who incited Dhingra to act on the mad idea of liberation by assassination bore the major responsibility for the act:

> I must say that those who believe and argue that such murders may do good to India are ignorant men indeed. No act of treachery can ever profit a nation. Even should the British leave in consequence of such murderous acts, who will then rule in their place? The only answer is: the murderers.... India can gain nothing from the rule of murderers—no matter whether they are black or white.[10]

Gandhi's critique of murder by influence could not have endeared him to Savarkar, to whose writings he was referring when he also said, "[Mr. Dhingra] was egged on to do this act by ill-digested reading of worthless writings."[11]

Gandhi had met Savarkar in 1906, when he stayed for a few days at India House.[12] He was familiar with Savarkar's influential book, *The First Indian War of Independence, 1857*, in which Savarkar used the Revolt of 1857 against the British to praise the "propensity in human nature" for "revolt, bloodshed, and revenge"[13]—encouraging what Gandhi, citing Wyllie's assassination, saw simply as "murderous acts." Gandhi also knew Savarkar's control over the young men in India House. He almost certainly suspected Savarkar's role in Wyllie's murder, as implied by his emphasizing that responsibility for the "mad idea" came from beyond the triggerman, Dhingra.

Gandhi also understood that someone in the shadows was responsible for the words the defendant used to proclaim the rightness of his assassinating Wyllie. Gandhi said: "[Mr. Dhingra's] defense of himself, too, appears to have been learnt by rote. It is those who incited him to this that deserve to be punished."[14]

On October 24, 1909, with the summer's assassination drama still in the air, Gandhi and Savarkar shared the same speakers' platform in London to present competing visions for India's future. They were the feature attractions in a subscription dinner at an Indian restaurant on the feast of Dussera, commemorating the victory of good over evil, Rama over Ravana, in the classic Hindu epic, *The Ramayana*. The dinner was the idea of Savarkar's militant students from India House.[15] They invited Gandhi into their lions' den, asking him to be their opening speaker, with Savarkar to follow.

Gandhi acknowledged later to a friend that the dinner "was given practically by the extremist Committee." He added, "I accepted the proposal unhesitatingly so that I might speak to those who might assemble there on the uselessness of violence for securing reform."[16] He had also laid down two conditions: that "the food should be purely vegetarian"[17] (which Gandhi himself would cook), and that "no controversial politics were to be touched upon."[18] The organizers agreed. Gandhi therefore happily peeled potatoes with the students in the kitchen on the afternoon of October 24, hours before he rose from his place at dinner to give his speech.[19]

Gandhi's talk drew on *The Ramayana* as a vision of suffering for the truth. The epic's main characters, he said, showed the way to freedom through suffering. He spoke of Rama, the incarnation of God, suffering in exile, Sita's pure endurance in captivity, and Lakshmana's practice of penitential disciplines. Their way of suffering for the truth, Gandhi believed, would liberate India "and be the source of a new victory of Truth over Falsehood."[20]

"When Indians learn to live in that manner," Gandhi said, "they can *from that instant* count themselves as free."[21] Gandhi saw freedom as already achieved by nonviolent means. A people became free in the present by suffering for the truth. They didn't have to wait for a colonial power to grant them freedom. A liberating, nonviolent means was already the end in the process of becoming.

Savarkar drew a different lesson from the same story. "Rama," he proclaimed, "established his ideal kingdom (Raja Raj) only after slaying Ravana, the symbol of oppression and injustice." Slaying Ravana was to be taken literally. One destroyed evil by destroying the evildoer. Savarkar's talk celebrated the fierce goddess Durga, the avenger, and the necessity of actually killing the evil one, Ravana.[22]

Without explicitly "touching on controversial politics," Gandhi and Savarkar had gone to the heart of the issue dividing them. They had engaged in a great debate that night not only over the meaning, violent or nonviolent, of Hindu mythology. They had also presented their very different means toward the goal of a free India.

For the next four decades, Gandhi's and Savarkar's own lives would embody their diametrically opposed visions of social change, with both visions culminating finally in Gandhi's assassination by Savarkar and his followers. In Savarkar's vision of *The Ramayana*, Ravana, the evil one who had to be slain, would turn out to be Gandhi. And Gandhi, as he had hoped, would die with the name of the incarnation of God, "Rama," on his lips, blessing his assassin. In Gandhi's vision of *The Ramayana*, Rama had to overcome Ravana in their final struggle not by killing the enemy evildoer but by lovingly giving his own life for the sake of truth.

By the time Gandhi left England to return to South Africa on November 13, 1909, he was deeply disturbed by the widespread acceptance of violence in the Indian independence movement. Savarkar and the residents of India House were extreme examples of a predominant attitude. "I have practically met no one," Gandhi said, "who believes that India can ever become free without resort to violence."[23]

Gandhi's dismay at Indians' acceptance of the school of violence moved him to write his most impassioned book, *Hind Swaraj*, aboard the *S.S. Kildonan Castle* on his way back to South Africa. His writing hand could not keep up with his ideas. He would write furiously with his right hand, then switch to his left, then back and forth again, completing the manuscript by the end of his ten-day voyage.

Hind Swaraj was Gandhi's radical manifesto for Indian freedom through nonviolence. *Swaraj* meant "self-rule." Gandhi saw Indian self-rule as, at root, a freedom from Western civilization (which he saw as a contradiction in terms). The West, he said bluntly, was a civilization of violence. For India to gain the end of freedom from its enslavement to the West, which alone would be true *swaraj,* it could do so only through nonviolent means. Otherwise Indians in their imitative rebellion would do nothing more than re-create the violent rule of the West, enslaving themselves all over again.

Gandhi developed his theme in the form of a dialogue between an "editor," who was himself, and a "reader," whose challenges came from Gandhi's confrontations with his opponents in London. Gandhi had heard the same words from Savarkar and his militant followers.[24] The essence of the editor-reader conflict, as Gandhi developed it, lay in the relation between means and ends:

EDITOR: If we become free, India is free. And in this thought you have a definition of Swaraj. It is Swaraj when we learn to rule ourselves. It is, therefore, in the palm of our hands. But such Swaraj has to be experienced, by each one for himself [or herself]. One drowning [person] will never save another. Slaves ourselves, it would be a mere pretension to think of freeing others. Now you will have seen that it is not necessary for us to have as our goal the expulsion of the English. If the English become Indianized, we can accommodate them. If they wish to remain in India along with their civilization, there is no room for them. It lies with us to bring about such a state of things.

READER: I cannot follow this. There seems little doubt that we shall have to expel the English by force of arms. The English are in the country like a blight which we must remove by every means.

EDITOR: We brought the English, and we keep them. Why do you forget that our adoption of their civilization makes their presence in India at all possible? Your hatred against them ought to be transferred to their civilization. But let us assume that we have to drive away the English by fighting, how is that to be done?

READER: At first, we shall assassinate a few English-men and strike terror; then, a few men who will have been armed will fight openly. We may have to lose a quarter of a million men, more or less, but we shall regain our land. We shall undertake guerilla warfare, and defeat the English.

EDITOR: That is to say, you want to make the holy land of India unholy. Do you not tremble to think of freeing India by assassination? What we need to do is to sacrifice ourselves. It is a cowardly thought, that of killing others. Whom do you suppose to free by assassination? Those who believe that India has gained by Dhingra's act and other similar acts in India make a serious mistake. Dhingra was a patriot, but his love was blind. He gave his body in a wrong way; its ultimate result can only be mischievous.

READER: Will you not admit that you are arguing against yourself? You know that what the English obtained in their own country they obtained by using brute force. I know you have argued that what they have obtained is use-less, but that does not affect my argument. They wanted useless things and they got them. My point is that their desire was fulfilled. What does it matter what means they adopted? Why should we not obtain our goal, which is good, by any means whatsoever, even by using violence?

EDITOR: It is perfectly true that they used brute force and that it is possible for us to do likewise, but by using similar means we can get only the same thing that they got. You will admit that we do not want that. Your belief that there is no connection between the means and the end is a great mistake. Through that mistake even men who have been considered religious have committed grievous crimes. Your reasoning is the same as saying that we can get a rose through planting a noxious weed. The means may be lik-ened to a seed, the end to a tree; and there is just the same inviolable connection between the means and the end as there is between the seed and the tree. We reap exactly as we sow.[25]

In *Hind Swaraj*, Gandhi was confronting the deadly illogic of Savarkar's assassination ethic, which upheld the murder of British officials as the means to the end of a free nation. In fact, choosing such means would result inexorably over the years, for those who did so, in the evolution of a new means and end, the murder of their opponent, Gandhi, for the sake of achieving an exclusively Hindu nation.

As Gandhi returned from London to the *satyagraha* movement in South Africa, Savarkar conspired to carry out an assassination in India. On December 21, 1909, a British magistrate in the Nasik District of India, A. M. T. Jackson, who was about to depart from his post, was shot to death at a farewell party being held in his honor. The sixteen-year-old assassin, Anant Kanhare, was tried and sentenced to death. The Browning pistol he had used to murder Jackson was traced back to Savarkar in London, who had smuggled it with other pistols through an intermediary into India. Kanhare's charged co-conspirators were seized with letters from Savarkar in their possession. The youthful assassin's motive was linked to Savarkar, whose older brother, Barbarao, had been arraigned for sedition by Magistrate Jackson. Barbarao was found guilty and received a life sentence. Kanhare stated at his trial that he had killed Jackson to avenge the elder Savarkar's sentence.[26]

Britain's Bombay government sent a telegraphic warrant to London for Vinayak Savarkar's arrest, charging him with sedition, distributing arms, and abetting the murder of Jackson. Savarkar surrendered to the authorities in London and was taken to Bombay, where he was tried and found guilty. In June 1911, he began serving a fifty-year sentence in the Cellular Jail at Port Blair on the Andaman Islands, notorious for its harsh conditions. Savarkar was forced to endure ten years in India's most brutal prison under British rule. Before the first year was over, he submitted a petition for clemency to the British. He followed it up with a 1913 petition in which he stated:

> If the Government in their manifold beneficence and mercy
> release me, I for one cannot but be the staunchest advocate

of constitutional progress and loyalty to the English government, which is the foremost condition of that progress.... Moreover my conversion to the constitutional line
would bring back all those misled young men in India and
abroad who were once looking up to me as their guide. I
am ready to serve the Government in any capacity they like,
for as my conversion is conscientious, so I hope my future
conduct would be. By keeping me in jail nothing can be got
in comparison to what would be otherwise. The Mighty
alone can afford to be merciful, and therefore where else
can the prodigal son return but to the parental doors of the
Government?[27]

While Savarkar was begging the British for release from prison
in the Andaman Islands, Gandhi was concluding his *satyagraha*
campaign in South Africa. When Gandhi moved back to India in
1915, he had to confront all over again the illogic of assassination. After living in South Africa for twenty-two years, he was
seen as a newcomer in the Indian independence movement. But
he didn't act like one. When confronted by students who insisted
that assassination was a necessary tactic for liberation from the
British, Gandhi was unbending in opposing them.

On March 31, 1915, Gandhi spoke to a huge gathering of
militant students in Calcutta. He told the students that assassinations were "absolutely a foreign growth in India." Those
wanting to terrorize India should know, he said, that he would
"rise against them." Yet he recognized the courage beneath their
commitment to terrorism—not in their willingness to kill, which
he rejected, but in their willingness to die, which he was prepared
to do himself, in nonviolent resistance. He told the advocates of
assassination that if they had a program for the country, they
should "place it openly before the public." He said: "If I am for
sedition, I must speak out for sedition. I must think out loud
and take the consequences.... If you are prepared to die, I am
prepared to die with you."[28]

Beginning in 1917 and extending into the 1920s and 1930s,
Gandhi did turn toward sedition against the British Empire,

did openly advocate it, and was prepared to die in the process. The beginning was his 1917 campaign with the peasants of the Champaran district to overcome the injustice of British share-cropping contracts.[29] When Gandhi arrived to investigate the situation, the British ordered him to get out of the area immediately, under the threat of jail. When Gandhi refused the order before a judge, thousands of supportive peasants nonviolently encircled the courthouse. The British backed off from a man who invited arrest and even death. A yearlong, grassroots, successful *satyagraha* campaign followed—a model for the entire country.

"What I did," Gandhi said, "was a very ordinary thing. I declared that the British could not order me around in my own country."[30] What made Gandhi's ordinary action extraordinary was its contagious character. The peasants of Champaran ceased bowing to injustice. They became as openly fearless as Gandhi toward the British occupation. A fearless example in the midst of the people—noncooperation with evil to the point of giving one's own life—marked the beginning of the end of British rule.

Gandhi described the choice of nonviolence over violence in his January 1930 article, "The Cult of the Bomb":

> It is not enough that we drive out Englishmen by making their lives insecure through secret violence. That would lead not to independence but to utter confusion. We can establish independence only by adjusting our differences through an appeal to the head and the heart, by evolving organic unity among ourselves, not by terrorizing or killing those who, we fancy, may impede our march, but by patient and gentle handling, by converting the opponent.

The alternative to violence was "to offer mass civil disobedience."[31]

Gandhi summed up his vision of freedom through nonviolence in three simple words: "Do or die." "Do or die" became his mantra of revolution to the end of his life: Resist injustice with one's whole life.[32] Do it lovingly. Resist nonviolently, openly, fearlessly. Suffer the consequences with joy, to the point of death: "Do or die."

Indians cast off their fear of the empire most dramatically in the nationwide *satyagraha* campaign initiated by the Salt March of 1930. Once again, the example of a fearless open defiance of imperial law was the catalytic event for a wider movement. Seventy-eight members of Gandhi's ashram marched with him for three weeks to the sea. On April 6, 1930, Gandhi "bent down and picked up a handful of mud, with natural salt in it,"[33] thereby breaking the law that gave the British a monopoly over the possession, use, and sale of India's salt. Gandhi's action sent a nonviolent signal to the nation.

In an interview that day, he said: "Now that a technical or ceremonial breach of the salt law has been committed, it is open to anyone who would take the risk of prosecution under the salt law to manufacture salt wherever he wishes and wherever it is convenient." He spoke especially to the poor in India's villages, whom the salt laws damaged most. Gandhi recommended civil disobedience to all but added: "It should be made absolutely clear to the villagers that this breach is to be open and in no way stealthy."[34]

The people followed Gandhi's example and counsel with massive nonviolent civil disobedience—taking salt from the sea, making salt, auctioning salt, selling salt, buying salt. Their law-breaking sent waves of Indians into the court system. Police tried to push back the tide by more and more arrests. The prisons overflowed.

The police awakened Gandhi in his hut at 1:30 a.m., May 5, and arrested him. He had written a letter earlier that night to the British viceroy, announcing that his next step would be to set out for Dharasana with his companions and take possession of the British-controlled salt works.[35] Gandhi went instead to prison, but the movement carried out his promised raid of the salt works.

On May 21, 1930, United Press correspondent Webb Miller reported to the world the encounter he witnessed at Dharasana between the British Empire's police and unarmed *satyagrahis*:

Prayers were said as white-clad volunteers knelt in the moonlight, and an impassioned speech by the poetess-leader, Mrs. Sarojini Naidu, opened the mass attack of 2,500 independence demonstrators ... on the Dharasana salt works.

The poetess, wearing a rough, home-spun robe and soft slippers, but no stockings, exhorted her followers to the raid.

"India's prestige is in your hands. You must not use any violence under any circumstances. You will be beaten but you must not resist: you must not even raise a hand to ward off blows.

"Although Gandhiji's body is in prison, his soul goes with you," she cried as she sent the volunteers to the attack.

The cry of "Gandhiji Jay!" answered her from the dark ranks of volunteers huddled together in the dim light of early morning.

The volunteers formed in columns, with their leaders carrying ropes and wire cutters. They advanced slowly towards the salt works.

Heaps of glistening salt surrounded by the barbed wire entanglements erected by police were the objective of the brief march. About 400 native Surat police stood inside and outside the entanglements. Several British officers directed the police, who had orders to prevent the assembly of more than five persons.

Manilal Gandhi, second son of Gandhi, walked along, the foremost of the marchers. As the throng drew near the salt pans, they commenced chanting the revolutionary slogan, "Inquilab Zindabad!" intoning the two words over and over.

The columns reached the salt works at 6:30 a.m. There were a few cheers and then the leaders, who had ropes, attempted to lasso the posts holding up the barbed wire, intending to uproot them. The police ran up and demanded that they disperse. The volunteers refused.

The column silently ignored the warning and slowly walked forward....

Suddenly, at a word of command, scores of native police rushed upon the advancing marchers and rained blows on their heads with their steel-shod lathis. Not one of the marchers even raised an arm to fend off the blows. They went down like ten-pins. From where I stood I heard the sickening whacks of the clubs on unprotected skulls. The waiting crowd of watchers groaned and sucked in their breaths in sympathetic pain at every blow.

Those struck down fell sprawling, unconscious or writhing with pain with fractured skulls or broken shoulders. In two or three minutes the ground was quilted with bodies. Great patches of blood widened on their white clothes. The survivors without breaking ranks silently and doggedly marched on until struck down. When every one of the first column had been knocked down, stretcher-bearers rushed up unmolested by the police and carried off the injured to a thatched hut which had been arranged as a temporary hospital.

Then another column formed while the leaders pleaded with them to retain their self-control. They marched slowly towards the police. Although everyone knew that within a few minutes he would be beaten down, perhaps killed, I could detect no signs of wavering or fear. They marched steadily with heads up, without the encouragement of music, of cheering or any possibility that they might escape serious injury or death. The police rushed out and methodically and mechanically beat down the second column. There was no fight, no struggle: the marchers simply walked forward until struck down. There were no outcries, only groans after they fell. There were not enough stretcher-bearers to carry off the wounded: I saw eighteen injured being carried off simultaneously, while forty-two still lay bleeding on the ground awaiting stretcher-bearers. The blankets used as stretchers were sodden with blood....

Several times the leaders nearly lost control of the waiting crowd. They rushed up and down, frantically pleading with and exhorting the intensely excited men to remember Gandhi's instructions. It seemed that the unarmed throng was on the verge of launching a mass attack upon the police. The British official in charge, Superintendent Robinson of Surat, sensed the imminence of an outbreak and posted twenty-five riflemen on a little knoll ready to fire. He came to me, inquiring my identity, and said: "You'd better move aside out of the line of shooting. We may be forced to open fire into the crowd." While we were talking, one of the Gandhiites, a young university student, ran up to Robinson, his face contorted by rage, tore open his cotton smock, exposing his bare breast, and shrieked: "Shoot me, shoot me! Kill me, it's for my country!" The leaders managed to calm the crowd.

The Gandhi men altered their tactics, marched up in groups of twenty-five and sat on the ground near the salt pans, making no effort to draw nearer. Led by a coffee-colored Parsi sergeant of police named Antia, a hulking, ugly-looking fellow, detachments of police approached one seated group and called up to them to disperse under the non-assemblage ordinance. The Gandhi followers ignored them and refused to even glance up at the lathis brandished threateningly above their heads. Upon a word from Antia, the beating commenced coldly, without anger. Bodies toppled over in threes and fours, bleeding from great gashes on their scalps. Group after group walked forward, sat down, and submitted to being beaten into insensibility without raising an arm to fend off the blows.

Finally the police became enraged by the non-resistance, sharing, I suppose, the helpless rage I had already felt at the demonstrators for not fighting back. They commenced savagely kicking the seated men in the abdomen and testicles. The injured men writhed and squealed in agony, which seemed to inflame the fury of the police, and the crowd again almost broke away from their leaders. The police then began dragging the sitting men by their arms or feet, sometimes for a hundred yards, and then throwing them into ditches. One was dragged into the ditch where I stood: the splash of his body doused me with muddy water. Another policeman dragged a Gandhi man to the ditch, threw him in, then belabored him over the head with his lathi. Hour after hour stretcher-bearers carried back a stream of inert, bleeding bodies.

Much of the time the stolid native Surat police seemed reluctant to strike. It was noticeable that when the officers were occupied on other parts of the line the police slackened, only to resume threatening and beating when the officers appeared again. I saw many instances of the volunteers pleading with the police to join them...

By eleven the heat reached 116 in the shade and the activities of the Gandhi volunteers subsided. I went back to the temporary hospital to examine the wounded. They lay in rows on the bare ground in the shade of an open, palm-thatched shed. I counted 320 injured, many still insensible with fractured skulls, others in writhing agony from kicks in the testicles and stomach. The Gandhi men had been able to gather only a few native doctors, who were doing the best they could with the inadequate facilities. Scores of the injured had received no treatment for hours and two had died.[36]

The raid Miller reported was resumed that evening, and four hundred more volunteers were injured. Two days later in the nearby *satyagraha* camp, after the police had evacuated it of all but a few of the *satyagrahis,* those remaining were confronted again by the police. One of that Gandhian remnant has described a final encounter with the police:

The officer returned in the afternoon of the 23rd and looked into with great care all the papers of the inmates of the camp. Some twenty policemen surrounded us. We were going on with our own work. As it was hot, we gave our police brethren a drink of cold fresh water. On the mornings of the 21st and 22nd, we had given them our blood as patiently and quietly. When the police came to drive us out of our place on the 22nd morning, they helped themselves to some fruits from our larder which we had stocked for our wounded soldiers. If they had only asked us, we should have given them the fruits gladly.[37]

Gandhi was once asked if he believed in the verse of the Sermon on the Mount, "If any man would take your coat, let him take your cloak as well." He answered:

In the verse quoted by you, Jesus put in a picturesque and telling manner the great doctrine of nonviolent noncooperation. Your noncooperation with your opponent is violent when you give a blow for a blow, and is ineffective in the long run. Your noncooperation is nonviolent when you give your opponent all in the place of just what he needs. You have disarmed him once for all by your apparent cooperation, which in effect is complete noncooperation.[38]

The *satyagrahis* of the 1930 civil disobedience campaign disarmed the British by nonviolent noncooperation, carried out in a spirit of love. As Indian casualties rose, British self-justification fell.

Gandhi's nonviolent signal to the nation with a handful of salt would have meant nothing, had not he and the members of his community been willing to do or die—had they not been willing to carry out their nonviolent resistance through long prison terms, beatings, and death itself. The salt *satyagraha* was a fulfillment of Gandhi's *swaraj* vision. It was freedom from the West's reliance on violence. It was freedom through nonviolence. In the process of entering the prison gates, marching into brute force, and giving up life itself, Indians became free, whereas the British lost the power of violence to subjugate the colonized. Violence had no power over those unafraid of it. The British never regained their domination over India. Gandhi's and his community's willingness to embrace suffering and death in loving resistance to the occupiers was the key to self-rule.

In his willingness to do or die, however, Gandhi was not immune to temptation. The worst temptation of his life may have been to precipitate his own death for the sake of *swaraj*. For decades Gandhi had prayed and disciplined himself to die nonviolently in obedience to God's will at any moment. In August 1942, when he felt the independence movement was approaching an impasse with Britain, he thought the moment to sacrifice his life was at hand.

Prime Minister Winston Churchill and his advisor, Secretary of State for India Leopold Amery, had decided to take pre-emptive action against Gandhi. Churchill and Amery were alarmed by Gandhi's demand that the British withdraw then from India, during World War II, or face nationwide civil resistance. The British leaders planned to arrest Gandhi and other Congress Party leaders as soon as the All-India Congress Committee passed a Quit India Resolution at its August 8 meeting in Bombay. The British War Cabinet had at one point even decided to deport Gandhi from India (probably to the British colony of Nyasaland in Southeast Africa) to control him more easily if he chose to fast in prison.[39] The War Cabinet finally chose instead to imprison Gandhi at the old Aga Khan Palace in India.

Gandhi knew the British were preparing to crush the independence movement as an intolerable wartime distraction. He felt their challenge was in turn an invitation to sacrifice everything for freedom. At the Bombay meeting he called on the Congress leaders to offer their lives for a free India:

> Here is a mantra, a short one, that I give you. You may imprint it on your hearts and let every breath of yours give expression to it. The mantra is: "Do or Die." We shall either free India or die in the attempt.... Let every man and woman live every moment of his or her life hereafter in the

consciousness that he or she eats or lives for achieving freedom and will die, if need be, to attain that goal.[40]

Gandhi wanted to be the first to act on his own words. As his
co-workers and even the British discerned, he was on the verge of
beginning a fast to the death, "if need be, to attain that goal," as
soon as he was arrested. He was even considering fasting without
water, which he knew would made the fast "short and swift."[41]

Gandhi's secretary, Mahadev Desai, feared that it would indeed
be short, swift, and to the death—a death that Desai thought the
British leaders, already under the stress of war, would have wel-
comed. Desai feared that "the government, desperate as it was,
would allow him to die in the ordeal" and "might even suppress
the news of Gandhiji's death."[42]

Even worse, Mahadev felt, was Gandhi's thinking, which
betrayed an uncharacteristic desperation and haste that were in
conflict with nonviolence. Desai convinced four other influential
Gandhi aides to join him in writing urgent pleas to their leader,
asking him to reconsider taking such a step. Mahadev wrote:

> On the previous day, you told Devadas [Gandhi's youngest
> son] and me, "All this is going to happen, you will not see
> me alive." I was quite agitated at that time. I felt that it was
> the impatience to see the result which was responsible in
> making it short and swift through the fast and I felt that
> you are indifferent about the fact that the world may or may
> not understand the significance of your stand....
>
> Please excuse me but I feel that the entire idea is delusory.
> Please remove from your mind the idea of short and swift.
> Just as mango trees do not grow in a hurry, sacrifices also
> cannot be offered in a hurry.[43]

Gandhi wrote only a short, noncommittal note in response to his
co-workers' urgent appeals.[44]

Mahadev's son, Narayan Desai, drawing on his father's diary,
has recorded the Congress Working Committee's opposition to
Gandhi's "intention of going on a fast unto death immediately

on being sent to prison. Jawaharlal [Nehru] had insisted that Bapu should not tie himself down by such a decision. Maulana said that such a step should be the last step. Pant voiced his fear that there would be violence and chaos because of it. Satyamurti felt that free India would need Bapu more than slave India. Prafulla Ghosh believed that a fast would be a suicide. Narendra Dev said that he was totally against a fast.... Sardar [Patel] had registered a strong protest.

"Gandhiji consoled the Working Committee by saying that he had not come to any decision."[45]

When the police came to arrest Gandhi and Desai in the early morning darkness of August 9, 1942, Narayan Desai, then seventeen years old, began to pack a few things for his father. Mahadev stopped him, saying: "There is no need for all these things. Bapu's fast hangs over my head like the sword of Damocles. If he undertakes a fast, the government may allow him to die. I am not going to remain alive to witness all that. I do not know if I would remain alive for more than a week in the jail."[46]

As Gandhi was being arrested, he told a friend who was apprehensive of his fasting that he did "not intend to announce a fast immediately."[47] The door to the fast remained open.

Mahadev Desai's own health was at a crossroads. When Mahadev entered the Aga Khan Palace prison with Gandhi, he was still recovering from a recent heart attack. The ashram had almost forgotten his weak heart, in view of the secretary's continuing his routine of devoted, energetic work for Gandhi.

Mahadev watched Gandhi anxiously in prison, fearing he would begin a fatal fast at any time. Mahadev was heard to say repeatedly, "My only prayer to God is 'please take me away before Bapu,' and God has never denied my prayer."[48] Fellow prisoners observed him living under a great strain. After six days Mahadev suddenly collapsed. He died in Gandhi's arms.

Gandhi, staring down and caressing Mahadev's head, shouted, "Mahadev! Get up! Mahadev!"[49]

Unlike Lazarus in response to Jesus' call, Mahadev did not rise up.

When asked later about his cry to his disciple, Gandhi said, "I am confident, that if even once Mahadev had opened his eyes and looked at me, he would have gotten up. Never once in his life did he not obey me. If my words had reached his ears, I am confident that he would have fought death and gotten up."[50]

Perhaps it was necessary, for Gandhi to feel the depth of his disciple's love, that Mahadev not open his eyes.

Narayan Desai believed that it was his father's death that made Gandhi turn away from a precipitous, possibly fatal fast. Pyarelal, Gandhi's other secretary and biographer, agreed that Mahadev's death stopped Gandhi's fast. He said, "When everyone's appeal failed to stop Gandhiji from undertaking the fast unto death, Mahadev succeeded. This is the only incident of its kind in Gandhiji's entire life according to my knowledge."[51]

Gandhi said simply, "Mahadev's sacrifice is not a small thing. He fully obeyed the call, 'Do or Die.' This sacrifice is bound to hasten India's day of liberation."[52]

For the sake of his teacher, the disciple had gone first.

In the summer of 1944, as the British were finally moving toward granting independence to India, Gandhi was harassed and threatened more than once by a group of men, some of whom would end up killing him three and a half years later.

The first incident of this kind occurred in July 1944, when Gandhi visited Panchgani, while recovering from illness after his release from his last time in prison. Twenty young men came into Panchgani on a chartered bus from Poona. Before Gandhi's prayer meeting at 5:30 p.m., the men marched around town, chanting anti-Gandhi slogans. Witnesses have given different versions of who the leader of this group was and of what he did at the prayer meeting that evening.

According to some witnesses, the leader of the group, Nathuram Godse, rushed toward Gandhi with a dagger, shouting, "Down with Gandhi!" Two Gandhi supporters overpowered and disarmed Godse, the same man who would shoot Gandhi to death on January 30, 1948. One of Gandhi's defenders was

D. Bhilare Guruji, who later became a Congress member of the legislature. Guruji recalled that when he and another man "grappled with Nathuram and wrestled him to the ground, Gandhi hailed them and instructed them not to be rough with the attacker. He wanted them to bring Nathuram to him so they could talk."[53] The police arrested Godse and his companions. "[Gandhi] asked Godse to spend eight days with him so that he could understand his point of view. Godse rejected this invitation and was allowed to go free by a magnanimous Gandhi."[54]

According to two police officers, it was the men as a group who disrupted the meeting by shouting slogans rather than their leader attacking Gandhi with a dagger. In the police version, the leader of the group was not Nathuram Godse but a friend of his, Narayan Apte.[55] The police identification of Apte as the leader was also significant, however, because it was Narayan Apte who would be sentenced to death with Godse in 1948, both for spearheading the murder of Gandhi.

Whichever of the two future assassins led the group in July 1944 into either attacking Gandhi or simply disrupting his meeting, the event was evidence of another man's shadow over Gandhi's future—Vinayak Damodar Savarkar, Gandhi's old nemesis from London. Both Nathuram Godse and Narayan Apte were disciples of Savarkar, now freed from prison with a new cadre of potential assassins.

Savarkar's petitions for clemency from the British Empire had borne fruit for the empire's "prodigal son," as he called himself in his 1913 appeal for mercy at "the parental doors of the Government."[56] During his solitary confinement at Port Blair, Savarkar's ideology turned away from rebellion against the empire. In September 1914, he wrote a letter to the British government in India expressing his hope for an Indo-British alliance based on a shared racial background that would transform the British Empire into "the Aryan Empire."[57] He wrote that he and other revolutionary leaders were now "ready and willing to be friends of the British Empire if it equipped India with a form of government vital for her freedom."[58]

In his discussions with other prisoners in 1921, Savarkar condemned Gandhi's nationwide campaign for an independence that was "to be won by the perverse doctrine of nonviolence and truth. The noncooperation movement for *swaraj* based on these twin principles was a movement without power and was bound to destroy the power of the country. It is an illusion, a hallucination, not unlike the hurricane that sweeps over a land only to destroy it. It is a disease of insanity, an epidemic and megalomania."[59]

In 1921 the British transferred Savarkar from the Andaman Islands to India's more moderate Ratnagiri Jail, where he became a jail librarian. In 1923 he was moved to Yeravda Jail, where he was appointed chief of a jail factory and was given permission to teach classes. He used his new freedom to change the minds of recently imprisoned *satyagrahis*.

"I began here," he wrote in his memoirs, "to criticize severely all these followers of Gandhi that their eyes might see clearly.... Winning Swaraj by [the spinning wheel], supporting the [Muslims'] Khilafat movement as the duty of the Hindus, and ridiculous definitions of nonviolence, I exploded them all by invincible logic and by an appeal to history."[60]

Gandhi was himself a Yeravda prisoner at the same time as Savarkar, jailed for sedition against the empire to which Savarkar now professed loyalty. Gandhi, a former loyal citizen of the empire, had become its foremost opponent, whereas Savarkar, the reputed rebel, promised the British he would abstain from political action in return for his release.

Savarkar pledged his allegiance to the empire in an interview at Yeravda with the British governor of Bombay, Sir George Lloyd. He accepted the governor's conditions for release that he not go outside Ratnagiri district and not engage in any political activities. Savarkar was released from Yeravda Jail on January 6, 1924.[61]

He justified his concessions to the British by identifying himself as a captured general, comparing himself to Lord Krishna: "Generals, as prisoners of war, cannot conduct the war and come

on the battlefield. They are let off on parole after signing the
pledge, like Lord Krishna, who agreed that he would not wield
any arm during the continuance of the war. And it is considered
no humiliation on their part to do so."[62]

Savarkar narrated in his memoirs a conversation he had with
fellow prisoners just before his release. Their farewell to him
seemed to return his mind to the subject of his 1909 London
debate with Gandhi: the meaning of Rama's victory over Ravana, the triumph of good over evil in *The Ramayana*. Savarkar's
supporters, he writes in retrospect, heralded his 1924 release in
epic terms, saying, "Savarkar, you have been an exile from your
country like Rama who went to the forest for fourteen years....
You have passed through similar trials, sorrows, and bereave-
ments." Savarkar says he responded:

> There is one great omission in this comparison. Rama went
> into exile, but Rama finished Ravana and won the battle. I
> have gone into exile and suffered, but Ravana is still alive. I
> shall feel myself free only when that is accomplished. With
> God's grace even that task will accomplish itself like many
> other minor things to which I have put my hand. Some day,
> sometime, that also will happen and you must realize the
> difference, and it must give you acute pain.[63]

Savarkar's prediction of his reenactment of Rama's victory
by killing Ravana, "some day, sometime," which "must give you
acute pain," was included in the English translation of his prison
memoirs. The translation, supervised by Savarkar, was published
in 1950,[64] two years after Gandhi's assassination was carried out
by a team of Savarkar's disciples.

After his release from jail in 1924 to the little seaside town of
Ratnagiri, Savarkar did in fact engage in political activities
but nothing that would disturb British authorities. In Ratnagiri
Jail, Savarkar had written what would become his best-known
book, *Hindutva: What Is a Hindu?,* an essay proclaiming his
newly adopted Hindu nationalist ideology. Outside jail he

became a master propagandist for his militantly anti-Muslim, culturally Hindu view of the world. The sharp division he was promoting between Hindus and Muslims was in effect an Indian endorsement of the British strategy of divide and rule.

One of Savarkar's early visitors in Ratnagiri in March 1925 was K. B. Hedgewar, a medical practitioner inspired by Savarkar's recently published *Hindutva*. Hedgewar consulted with Savarkar on how to implement his Hindu nationalist vision. Following their discussion, Hedgewar founded the Rashtriya Swayamsevak Sangh (RSS), "the Organization of National Volunteers,"[65] whose innocuous name covered an organization that consciously copied the strategy of Mussolini's fascist Blackshirts.[66] The RSS would become infamous by terrorizing Muslims to gain political power in India at the end of the twentieth century.

As Savarkar began creating a new ideological following, Gandhi paid him a friendly visit at his home in Ratnagiri in 1927. It was the last time they would ever meet. When Gandhi was about to leave, he said to Savarkar, "It is clear that we disagree on some problems. But I hope you have no objection to my experiments." Savarkar said, "You will be making the experiments at the cost of the nation."[67]

In 1929, Vinayak Godse, a postal worker, was transferred to Ratnagiri. Three days after the Godse family's arrival in town, Vinayak's nineteen-year-old son, Nathuram, visited Savarkar for the first time. As Nathuram's younger brother and co-conspirator in Gandhi's murder, Gopal, has written, Nathuram then "went to [Savarkar] often.... Nathuram gladly undertook the work of copying the writings of Veer [meaning "brave"] Savarkaar."[68] "Impressed by Nathuram's devotion, Savarkar appointed him as his secretary."[69] Nathuram also joined the RSS, eventually heading the "academic department" of one of its branches.[70] Nathuram Godse had discovered his lifelong vocation—following, promoting, and carrying out Savarkar's teaching.

In the 1930s, Savarkar helped create the anti-Muslim, military-oriented Hindu Mahasabha organization. He was Mahasabha president from 1937 through 1944. When the Second World War began, Savarkar urged Hindu youths to join the British-led

armed forces so they could be "re-born into a martial race."[71]
His 1940s slogan wed Hindu nationalism with the war effort:
"Hinduise all politics and militarize Hindudom."[72]

A second incident in 1944 involving Savarkar's followers again
foreshadowed Gandhi's assassination. It happened two months
after the first—in September 1944—when Gandhi was about to
hold what he hoped would be unifying talks with the Muslim
leader, Muhammad Ali Jinnah. Another group of young men,
including Nathuram Godse, came to Gandhi's Sevagram Ashram,
vowing publicly to use any means necessary to stop Gandhi from
meeting with Jinnah. The men picketed the ashram's gates, preparing themselves to block Gandhi's departure for the meeting.
When the police arrested and searched the men, they found on
one "a sharp knife, 7½ inches long, concealed on his person."[73]

Gandhi's secretary, Pyarelal, has recounted in his biography
of Gandhi a conversation that took place that day between an
arresting officer and the man found with the concealed knife:

> The officer said in a joking manner, "At any rate you
> have had the satisfaction of becoming a martyr."
>
> The man replied quickly, "No, that will be when some-
> one assassinates Gandhiji."
>
> The officer said, "Why not leave it to the leaders to settle
> it among themselves? For instance, Savarkar might come
> and do the job."
>
> The man said, "That will be too great an honor for
> Gandhiji. The *jamadar* [pointing to the man beside him]
> will be quite enough for the purpose."[74]

Pyarelal comments: "The person referred to as *jamadar* [mean-
ing "watchman"] was his fellow-picketer—Nathuram Vinayak
Godse"—Gandhi's future murderer.[75]

The context of Gandhi's murder, as actually carried out by
Godse, was that on January 12, 1948, Gandhi announced at
his prayer meeting in Delhi that the next day he would begin a fast

to death. "I yearn for heart friendship," he said, "between Hindus, Sikhs, and Muslims."[76] For the past year and a half, Hindus, Sikhs, and Muslims had been slaughtering one another, leading up to and following the British government's partition in August 1947 of what had been one India into the two newly independent countries of India and Pakistan. A vast number of Hindus and Sikhs had been purged from Pakistan, and a comparable number of Muslims from India. Hundreds of thousands on both sides were dead, dying, or fleeing persecution from their enemies.

Gandhi was dismayed. He said,

> There was a time when nobody believed that India could win her independence by nonviolence. But now that independence has become a reality, we are bidding fair to say goodbye to nonviolence.... If India has no further use for Ahimsa, can she have any for me? I would not in the least be surprised if in spite of all the homage that the national leaders pay to me, they were one day to say, "We have had enough of this old man. Why does not he leave us alone?"[77]

In October 1946, Gandhi had been tempted to despair. Word reached him that Muslims were massacring Hindus in the majority Muslim district of Noakhali in East Bengal. Hindus were in turn massacring Muslims in the majority Hindu province of Bihar. Gandhi's lifelong vision of Hindu-Muslim unity was disappearing in darkness. He resolved to go immediately to Noakhali.

"I do not know what I shall be able to do there," he told a friend, "All I know is that I won't be at peace with myself unless I go there." His thought was simply to go to the people of Noakhali, Hindus and Muslims alike, and to do God's will. Unless it could be translated into action, the thought would be powerless. "But one active thought," he said, "proceeding from the depths, in its nascent purity and endowed with all the undivided intensity of one's being, can become dynamic and make history."[78]

Noakhali was a densely inhabited region, forty miles square, in a delta accessible only by waterways, overgrown footpaths, and precarious bridges.[79] The population included 1,800,000 Muslims and 400,000 Hindus. The minority Hindus were landowners and professionals. They had ignored grievances from Muslim workers who, incensed by tales of Hindus killing Muslims elsewhere, carried out savage attacks on Noakhali's Hindus.[80]

Gandhi visited the most affected villages. They followed a pattern—a few clusters of Hindu families' huts that were burnt to the ground, surrounded by a large number of Muslim dwellings. Most of the Hindus in such areas had been killed, with the charred remains of corpses and bones lying about. Other Hindus had fled. Those remaining had blank faces. They were living in shock and terror. Most of the Muslims met Gandhi's questions with total denial. No one was willing to accept responsibility for the horrors, whose evidence was all around.

Yet while Gandhi was seeing how the majority Muslims butchered Hindus in Bengal, he was hearing reports of how the majority Hindus butchered Muslims in Bihar.[81]

At his November 18, 1946, prayer gathering, Gandhi described the fear he encountered everywhere in Noakhali and what could overcome it:

> The more I go about in these parts, the more I find that your worst enemy is fear. The terrorist as well as the terrorized is equally its victim. It eats into their vitals. The former fears something in his victim. It may be the latter's religion, which is different from the terrorist's, or the latter's riches....
>
> But there has never been and never will be a man who can intimidate one who has cast out fear from his heart because God is always by the side of the fearless. If we make God our sole refuge, all our fears will vanish. Unless you cultivate fearlessness, there will never be any peace in these parts for the Hindus or for the Muslims.[82]

Fearlessness meant the need to walk alone through a domain of terror. The thought required a program of action to combat terror, which Gandhi shared with his co-workers. He invited the handful of *satyagrahis* who were with him to live fearlessness by fanning out one by one to the villages of terrorized Noakhali. Each would live alone, in the midst of the perpetrators and survivors of mass murder. They were to "make themselves hostages for the safety and security of the Hindus in that village."[83] They would clean up the burnt and vandalized property, rebuild homes, serve the community, and gradually restore mutual trust between Hindus and Muslims. They would seek the support of Muslims for the safe, peaceful return of Hindus who had fled in terror. For the sake of fearlessness, each *satyagrahi* would carry out his or her constructive work alone, dependent on the help of those in the village.[84] Their purpose was to dispel terror in Noakhali by a fearless nonviolence.

A skeptical member of Gandhi's party said, "How can you reason with people who are thirsting for your blood? Only the other day two of our workers were murdered."

"I know," Gandhi said, "But to quell the rage is our job."

He wrote to a friend: "The work I am engaged in here may be my last act. If I return from here alive and unscathed, it will be like a new birth to me. My Ahimsa is being tried here through and through as it was never before."[85]

After living in the village of Srirampur, in January 1947, Gandhi began a day-by-day pilgrimage walking through the terrorized region. In seven weeks, he visited 47 villages, walking 116 miles.[86]

Each morning at 7:30 as the sun began to rise, Gandhi would set out, singing the theme of his pilgrimage, from poet Rabindranath Tagore's song "Walk Alone":

Walk alone.
If they answer not to thy call, walk alone;
If they are afraid and cower mutely facing the wall,
O thou of evil luck,
Open thy mind and speak out alone.

If they turn away and desert you when crossing the
    wilderness,
O thou of evil luck,

Trample the thorns under thy tread,
And along the blood-soaked track travel alone.

If they do not hold up the light
When the night is troubled with storm,
O thou of evil luck,
With the thunder-flame of pain ignite thine own heart
And let it burn alone.[87]

Walking against a background of sky and vegetation, Gandhi could be seen crossing the *shankos* of Noakhali, narrow bamboo bridges held high on poles. At the age of seventy-seven, he initially needed help to negotiate the dangerously slippery bridges. But he practiced four times a day at a lower height, saying, "I must cross it alone."[88] He soon became a secure lone walker across each *shanko* (as in the picture on this book's cover).

He experienced other obstacles—human excrement left on his paths, an occasional person spitting in his face, the constant threat of assassination.[89] As he passed by glimmering fields each morning, he greeted Muslim peasants on their way to work.[90]

Despite the cautions of hostile leaders, who feared Gandhi, the people responded to the pilgrim in their midst. They joined him in his evening prayer meetings.[91] Even there, however, Gandhi faced the threat of death. He resolved such conflicts without relying on police, as witnessed by a reporter who wrote:

[Gandhi] arranged with the government that no one should be arrested in his prayer meetings. One Muslim came and was unaffected by the Mahatma. He grabbed the Mahatma by the throat and choked him till he was blue in the face. In the midst of it the Mahatma kept on smiling and even laughing. The absence of resistance and even of resentment so unnerved the attacker that he desisted. Later he came and fell at the Mahatma's feet and begged forgiveness for what he had done.[92]

Step by step, Gandhi's pilgrimage into a power beyond terror, multiplied by the constructive work of his co-workers in their villages, made an impact on Noakhali. His presence nurtured courage in both Hindus and Muslims.

In a survey of pre-partition violence, Justice G. D. Khosla described Gandhi's nonviolent counterforce in Noakhali: "[Gandhi] brought the light of reason and sanity to mad Noakhali. Large numbers of Muslims came forward and pledged to protect the Hindu minorities. Confidence once again returned, the Hindus cast away their fears and began to go back to their homes."[93]

The fiery test of Noakhali did not kill nonviolence. It forged Gandhi's even deeper faith in the power of *satyagraha*.[94] He then moved on to Bihar, and eventually Calcutta and Delhi, to combat there the terrorism of Hindu massacres of Muslims, in a cycle that could be ended only by nonviolence.

From Noakhali to Bihar, Calcutta, and Delhi, Gandhi had become a nonviolent lightning rod, absorbing on the one hand the violence of Muslims, in areas they wanted purged of Hindus for Pakistan, and elsewhere the violence of Hindus who wanted an India purged of Muslims. At the center of the storm in Delhi where Hindus were dominant, Gandhi was attacked for favoring Muslims, as was true in that context. He always favored the minority. He always identified with the most vulnerable, those whom Jesus of Nazareth called "the least of these."[95] Sometimes Muslim, sometimes Hindu or Sikh, and always the "untouchables" or *Harijans* ("Children of God," as Gandhi called those at the bottom of the caste system), the identity of "the least of these" depended on political and social circumstances. Gandhi lived and died with those at the bottom.

Having become in January 1948 the Muslims' defender in Delhi, India's Hindu-dominated capital, Gandhi was in deepening danger. The Hindu right had allied itself with elements of Gandhi's own Congress Party. Savarkar's followers held cabinet and administrative positions in the government.[96] Hindu Mahasabha and RSS extremists had also infiltrated India's security forces. Key police officials were more committed to an exclusively Hindu nation than they were to Gandhi's democratic ideal of a diverse, secular union.[97] They could not be counted on to protect the life of a presumably pro-Muslim *satyagrahi,* when he was attacked by forces the police sympathized with. The state police provided the context of Gandhi's murder.

Gandhi knew he was living out his life in a ring of fire. He kept telling co-workers, "Don't you see? I am mounted on my funeral pyre." Could they not see the signs of the time? They were a sign of his death. He emphasized his warning by saying, "You should know it is a corpse that is telling you this."[98]

The evil of partition set the stage for his assassination. It had happened with the participation of his own disciples, Jawaharlal Nehru and Vallabhbhai Patel, as they led India's interim government in the months before independence.

When the British announced in February 1947 their intention to quit India, they began a transfer of power that proved to be just as divisive as their imperial rule. By saying one thing in negotiations with Gandhi's Congress Party leaders on the transfer of power and another in confidence with Muhammad Ali Jinnah and the Muslim League, the British perpetuated their divide-and-rule strategy. It resulted in the partition of India and the creation of Pakistan.[99]

After Gandhi undertook his Noakhali pilgrimage in the first two months of 1947, he discovered that Patel and Nehru had without his knowledge surrendered to Jinnah's violent campaign for a separate Muslim state, reinforced by British administrative pressures favoring partition.[100] Nehru's and Patel's endorsement of partition, with its concession of Pakistan, enabled Gandhi's former lieutenants and other Congress Party leaders to achieve unimpeded power in India's independent government, after experiencing months of obstruction by Muslim League representatives in the interim government. The Muslim leaders' departure for the separate state of Pakistan left Nehru and Patel feeling free at last to rule India. When the British revealed their secretly determined borders of India and Pakistan, and millions of Hindus, Sikhs, and Muslims fled a mutual genocide, Gandhi struggled for ways to overcome the horrifying consequences of partition.

Gandhi's Delhi fast for Hindu-Muslim unity in the wake of partition then provided the rationale for a murderous decision already made by Savarkar and his disciples. Gandhi had been their target for years. But never had the time seemed more opportune for them to kill him. The assassins would now blame Gandhi for partition, seeking by propaganda to justify their murdering him as an act in defense of Hindu nationalism. Nathuram Godse and Narayan Apte would be Savarkar's lead assassins, after assembling a team blessed and guided by their master. Godse was now the editor, and Apte the publisher, of a newspaper in Poona, the *Agrani*—or as it was renamed, the *Hindu Rashtra*[101]—that propagated Savarkar's militant Hindu-ism. Their relationship to Savarkar was total obeisance. Apte summed it up in his notes for a speech on Savarkar's Hindutva ideology:

> Leader:—Savarkar
> Policy:—Obeying one leader.
> What is meant by one leadership? Relations.
> To carry out orders received from above.[102]

Two days before Gandhi announced his Delhi fast, Godse and Apte had already ordered the arsenal they would use for their assassination plot. On January 10, they placed the order with Digambar Badge, an arms salesman in Poona. They told Badge to have the necessary explosives, revolvers, and hand grenades delivered to them by January 14 at the Hindu Mahasabha office in Bombay.[103] Savarkar had moved to Bombay, where the assassins would seek their mentor's final instructions and blessing. On the night of January 12, when Godse and Apte read the announce-ment of Gandhi's fast from their teleprinter, they set January 20 as their target date for murdering the mahatma.[104]

On January 13, the first day of his final fast, Gandhi said, "I shall terminate the fast only when peace has returned to Delhi. If peace is restored to Delhi it will have effect not only on the whole of India but also on Pakistan. When that happens, a Muslim will be able to walk around in the city all by himself."[105]

While Gandhi fasted at the Delhi home of his industrialist friend, G. D. Birla, the members of the Indian government's cabinet met nearby to reconsider a deeply controversial issue. When the British had granted India and Pakistan their independence the previous August, Pakistan was owed fifty-five million rupees from undivided India's cash balance. The Indian government withheld payment, however, while the two new countries fought that fall over the disputed border region of Kashmir. The cabinet members knew Gandhi was disturbed by India's failure to pay Pakistan. On the other hand, they were appalled by the possibility of funding what they saw as Pakistan's invasion of Kashmir. Gandhi's fast to the death for the sake of Hindu-Muslim unity was pushing them beyond their psychic and political limits.

On January 14, the second day of Gandhi's fast, Godse and Apte traveled from Poona to the Hindu Mahasabha office in Bombay, where they met Badge and his servant Shankar. Badge had brought a heavy khaki bag. It contained two explosive guncotton (cellulose nitrate) slabs, fuses, primers, and five hand grenades. Badge, Apte, and Godse walked from the Hindu Mahasabha office to Savarkar's home. While Badge waited outside, Apte and Godse took the bag of explosives and went into the house.[106]

The next day Apte told Badge "Savarkar had decided that Gandhiji, Jawaharlal Nehru and Suhrawardy should be 'finished' and had entrusted that work to them."[107]

Suhrawardy?

Who was the Suhrawardy who Savarkar said should be "finished" along with Gandhi and Prime Minister Nehru?

Gandhi's deep belief in people who opposed him was exemplified by his persistent friendship with Shaheed Suhrawardy, the Muslim League's Chief Minister of Bengal in 1946-47.

When Gandhi made his lonely pilgrimage of reconciliation through the Noakhali district of Bengal in 1947, Chief Minister Suhrawardy told him to go elsewhere. Suhrawardy downplayed

Muslim violence against the minority Hindus, whose evidence of persecution Gandhi saw at first hand. Suhrawardy was notorious among Hindus for his government's complicity in the Great Calcutta Killing of August 1946, when 4,000 people were killed and 11,000 injured in four terrible days of Muslim League "direct action" and Hindu retaliation.[108] In the minds of Hindus, Shaheed Suhrawardy was their archenemy,[109] thought to be the man most responsible for the Great Calcutta Killing.[110] Yet Gandhi insisted on the responsibility and redemption of both sides, excluding no one. He reached out to Suhrawardy, challenging but not condemning him.

At their first meeting after the Calcutta mayhem, Gandhi asked Suhrawardy with a teasing smile, "How is it, Shaheed Sahib, everybody calls you the chief of the goondas [thugs]? Nobody seems to have a good word to say about you!"

Suhrawardy jabbed back: "Mahatmaji, don't people say things about you, too, behind your back?"

"That may be," Gandhi laughed. "Still there are at least some who call me Mahatma. But I have not heard a single person calling you, Shaheed Suhrawardy, a Mahatma!"

Suhrawardy said, "Mahatmaji, don't believe what people say about you in your presence!"[111]

Although Suhrawardy could banter with his friend Gandhi, he was unwilling to accept any responsibility for the Calcutta killing. He also dismissed Gandhi's frank letters stating that the chief minister's police were conniving with Muslim rioting against Hindus in Noakhali. Suhrawardy said confidently, "My police are my eyes and ears." Based on his own experience, Gandhi said, "As eyes and ears, the police are blind and deaf."[112]

As Suhrawardy's defensive letters became more belligerent, Gandhi addressed him in a response as "My dear Shaheed," then shared a memory of meeting him as a much younger man—an aspiring *satyagrahi* at a spinning wheel. Gandhi recalled encouraging his earnest efforts, "though you were unable to pull an even or fine thread. And then, if I remember rightly, when I applied to you some distant adjective of affection, you corrected me by saying that you felt as a son to me. I would like to think still that you are the same Shaheed and to feel proud that my son has become the Chief Minister of Bengal."[113]

In May 1947, a more subdued Suhrawardy, who was losing power, came to Gandhi to seek his support for the chief minister's scheme to unite an independent Bengal. Gandhi said, "A new Bengal cannot be born in utter disregard of the past. When the past is so full of wrongs, how can people believe in the sincerity of the new proposal unless past wrongs are set right?"[114]

Gandhi's aide Nirmal Bose raised the question of a police failure to investigate a murder. When Suhrawardy again disclaimed any personal responsibility, Gandhi broke in and said, "Yes, you are responsible not only for that murder but for every life lost in Bengal, whether Hindu or Muslim."

Suhrawardy recoiled. He said, "No, it is you who are responsible for it, for you have denied justice to the Mussulmans."

Gandhi said, "Don't talk rot."[115]

Suhrawardy returned to Gandhi the next day to re-present his case for a united sovereign Bengal. He admitted, "Its chief obstacle is that no Hindu will listen to me today."

Gandhi responded to his honesty with a unique offer of help. He said, "I will act as your secretary. I will live under the same roof with you. I will see to it that the Hindus at least give you a patient hearing. Are you prepared to accept the offer?"

For once, Suhrawardy was too stunned to reply. He departed quickly. As Bose left him at his car, Suhrawardy mumbled, "What a mad offer! I have to think ten times before I can fathom its implications."[116]

Three months later, when Gandhi stopped in Calcutta, they met again. Suhrawardy's Bengal scheme had been shot down by both Hindus and Muslims. His term as chief minister was expiring. Hindu-Muslim rioting had become chronic in Calcutta. It was August 11, 1947, four days before Britain would grant India and Pakistan independence, while partitioning them. As Muslims fled India for Pakistan, Calcutta's remnant Muslims suffered Hindu retaliation for last year's Great Calcutta Killing.

Suhrawardy pleaded with Gandhi to remain in Calcutta. It

was a burning city. Would he prolong his stay until real peace could be restored?[117]

Gandhi said, "I will remain if you and I are prepared to live together. This is my second offer to you. We shall have to work as long as every Hindu and Mussulman in Calcutta does not safely return to the place where he was before. We shall continue in our effort until our last breath."[118]

Suhrawardy knew Gandhi was serious. The Muslim leader was being invited into a nonviolent fire. The consequences of his saying yes would be life changing.

Gandhi gave him time to deliberate. "Go home and consult your daughter," he said, adding what his prospective disciple already knew and feared, "The old Suhrawardy will have to die."[119]

The next day Suhrawardy sent word of his decision back to Gandhi. He said yes.[120]

On August 13, Gandhi and Suhrawardy moved together into an old abandoned Muslim mansion in the Calcutta slum of Beliaghata. That first night a crowd of angry young Hindu men broke doors and windows, pushed through the house, and surrounded Gandhi. They said they didn't want any of his sermons on *ahimsa*. They told him to get out. Gandhi engaged them in dialogue.

He asked, "How can I, who am a Hindu by birth, a Hindu by creed, and a Hindu of Hindus in my way of living, be an 'enemy' of Hindus?"[121]

The next day, the young men returned for a long talk with Gandhi, as Suhrawardy sat beside him. When the youth left, they promised to win over their friends for reconciliation with Muslims.

Gandhi had chosen the perfect companion for his Calcutta experiment with truth. The Hindus' symbol of evil, Shaheed Suhrawardy, was at the heart of Calcutta consciousness. As Gandhian scholar Dennis Dalton put it, "No individual could have better disarmed Muslim suspicion and also attracted the hostilities of the Hindus, drawing them into the 'experiment' where they could be neutralized nonviolently."[122]

On August 14, the eve of India's and Pakistan's independence, over ten thousand people jammed the grounds for Gandhi's prayer meeting. "Where is Suhrawardy?" they shouted. Gandhi said that to avoid provoking them, Suhrawardy had stayed in the house, but that he would be at the next day's prayer meeting.

After Gandhi went inside, the people stoned the house, calling for Suhrawardy. Gandhi threw open a shutter. He quieted the crowd, brought Suhrawardy to the window, and placed his hand on his friend's shoulder.

As Suhrawardy tried to speak, a voice in the crowd demanded: "Are you not responsible for the Great Calcutta Killing?"

Suhrawardy said, "Yes, we all are."

"Will you answer my question, please?"

"Yes, it was *my* responsibility."

Suhrawardy's confession was a moment of grace. "It was," Gandhi said later, "a turning point. It had a cleansing effect. I could sense it."[123]

On August 15, Independence Day, crowds of Hindus and Muslims processed together through the streets of Calcutta. In their mutual celebration, they acted as if they had forgotten their battles. Gandhi doubted if they had. As he waited for the bubble to burst, what India was calling "the miracle of Calcutta" lasted for two and a half weeks.

On the night of August 31, Calcutta's peace ended where it had begun—in Gandhi's presence. A riotous crowd broke into the Beliaghata house, awakening Gandhi. Furious Hindus had carried in a bandaged man they claimed was the victim of Muslim violence. They wanted to put their hands on Suhrawardy (who was away) to avenge their fellow Hindu. Gandhi got up from his sleeping mat. Restrained by anxious co-workers, he tried to walk into the angry crowd, as it demanded revenge on Suhrawardy.

Gandhi cried out, "What is all this? Kill me! Kill me, I say! Why don't you kill me?"[124] They almost did. Someone swung a lathi stick at him. It barely missed his head, smashing against the wall. A brick aimed at him struck and hurt a friend. "What was attempted," Gandhi said later, "was an indifferent imitation of lynch law."[125]

Gandhi said finally in a husky voice, as much to himself as to the crowd, "My God asks me, 'Where do you stand?' I am deeply pained. Is this the reality of the peace that was established on August 15th?"[126]

The next day just outside the house, murder occurred. Two Muslim men were killed, while being transported in the back of a truck to a safer locality. Hand grenades were thrown on them from a nearby roof. Gandhi went out and prayed by the bodies. He was shaken by the spreading violence in the city. By nightfall fifty had been killed and more than three hundred injured. Gandhi toured the devastated areas.[127] He began to fast that night, announcing it to the press.[128] He said, "It will be 'do or die.' Either there will be peace or I shall be dead."[129]

On the first day of his fast, Calcutta continued to riot. Two *satyagrahis* who tried to subdue the violence were killed. Gandhi celebrated their lives and continued his fast. By the second and third days, the people were feeling Gandhi's pain. Peaceful processions crossed the city.

On the fourth day, leaders of the killing groups came to Gandhi. They surrendered weapons, beseeching him to end his fast. They would gladly undergo any penalty Gandhi would give them.[130]

Gandhi said, "My penalty for you is that you should go immediately among the Muslims and assure them full protection. The moment I am convinced that real change of heart has taken place, I will give up the fast."[131]

On the night of September 4, Suhrawardy brought in a delegation representing all the communities of Calcutta.[132] Gandhi told them he would end the fast only if they were willing to give their lives to prevent a return to violence. The leaders retired to the next room. In half an hour they came back, having signed a pledge that promised Gandhi: "Now that peace and quiet have been restored in Calcutta once again, we shall never allow communal strife in the city and shall strive unto death to prevent it."[133]

As Gandhi received the pledge, more gang leaders trying to save his life arrived in a truck. It was filled with hand grenades and arms to be surrendered to him. Gandhi decided Calcutta's turn toward peace was real. Suhrawardy handed him a glass of one ounce of sweet lemon juice, and he broke his fast.[134]

Two days later at the prayer meeting, Suhrawardy announced he would be joining Gandhi on his next mission of peace. He said he would be going with him to the Punjab—but as it turned out, to Delhi. He said, "I have put myself unreservedly under Mahatmaji's orders. Hereafter I will carry out his biddings."[135]

Suhrawardy would work with Gandhi for the five months left until his assassination. That fall Suhrawardy shuttled between India and Pakistan, acting as Gandhi's intermediary in his futile appeals to Jinnah for mutual cooperation.

In October, Gandhi wrote another message of costly grace to Suhrawardy: "You and I have to die in the attempt to make [Hindus and Muslims] live together as friends and brothers, which they are."[136]

In the years following Gandhi's assassination, Shaheed Suhrawardy would become a leader of pro-democracy movements in Pakistan. In 1956, as the National Assembly's opposition leader, he helped create the constitution of Pakistan.[137] He then became the country's prime minister from September 1956 to October 1957.

After he left office, the next government suspended the constitution and declared martial law. In 1958 Suhrawardy refused to support Ayub Khan's dictatorship. In 1959 the government banned him from politics. As he continued to voice his dissent, in 1962 he was charged with "anti-state activities."[138] He was imprisoned in solitary confinement for six months.

Upon his release in August 1962, Suhrawardy courageously launched a movement in resistance to Ayub Khan's military dictatorship. His goal was to restore the 1956 constitution and a parliamentary democracy.

While the pro-democracy movement was growing, its leader Shaheed Suhrawardy died suddenly on December 5, 1963, in a hotel room in Beirut, Lebanon. Expiring "under unusually mysterious circumstances,"[139] he was possibly "poisoned or gassed in his bedroom."[140]

Mohammad Talukdar, the editor of Shaheed Suhrawardy's memoirs, has noted two ominous statements from the powerful in Pakistan shortly before Suhrawardy's death. The first came from Zulfikar Ali Bhutto, then Pakistan's foreign minister, who passed on to Suhrawardy through a mutual friend the warning: "Tell Suhrawardy not to try and return to Pakistan. Otherwise I shall make sure personally that he never sets foot on its soil."[141] Bhutto's threat was followed by a caution from an officer in Pakistan's Central Intelligence Department to Suhrawardy's son: "Tell your father to take great care of himself. The word is going round that they are out to get him." Three days later his father was dead.[142]

The conflicted Muslim leader, who with Gandhi risked his life to save Calcutta from another massacre, died trying to save democracy in Pakistan.

On his way to that end, which would have made Gandhi proud of his "son," Shaheed Suhrawardy became with his spiritual father a target for assassination in Delhi.

The assassins' intention to kill Prime Minister Nehru, as well as Gandhi and Suhrawardy, would be confirmed by Nathuram Godse. After his arrest for murdering Gandhi, Godse confessed their further targeting of Nehru to G. K. Handoo, Nehru's head of security. As Handoo testified in the Indian government's later re-examination of Gandhi's assassination, "Godse admitted to me that their next target would have been Prime Minister Nehru."[143]

Savarkar and his co-conspirators planned to use the suffering of refugees from Pakistan to justify the murder of Gandhi—and of his co-workers, Nehru and Suhrawardy, if the team of assassins could carry out Savarkar's orders to "finish them" as well.[144] The assassins could thereby deliver a mortal blow to a fledgling democracy. If the assassins managed to kill Gandhi and Nehru, they would have eliminated the newly independent country's two greatest leaders. Killing Suhrawardy, a catalyst for Hindu-

Muslim reconciliation, would have been a bonus. Savarkar's anti-Muslim Hindu Mahasabha and RSS movement could then try to seize power in the resulting crisis. The Hindus and Sikhs displaced from their homes in Pakistan resented Gandhi's support, backed by Nehru, of the besieged Muslim minority in India. By killing Gandhi, and possibly Nehru and Suhrawardy, Savarkar hoped to ignite an anti-Gandhi inferno in the Hindu and Sikh refugee camps.

As if confirming the conspirators' plans, that same night in Delhi a group of Sikhs who had suffered from Muslim violence gathered outside Birla House. They chanted: "Blood for blood!" "We want revenge!" "Let Gandhi die!"

Prime Minister Nehru was about to depart in his car from a meeting with Gandhi. Hearing the chants, he got out of the car, ran at the demonstrators, and yelled, "Who dares to shout 'Let Gandhi die'? Let him who dares repeat those words in my presence! He will have to kill me first!" The chanters scattered.

From his bed, Gandhi heard the commotion outside. He asked, "What are they shouting?"

"They are shouting, 'Let Gandhi die.'"

"How many are they?"

"Not many."

Gandhi sighed and prayed, "Rama, Rama, Rama."[145]

On the third day of the fast, January 15, Gandhi's doctors warned that his kidney was failing. Too weak to walk to the prayer ground, Gandhi had to speak from his bed into a microphone.

He reiterated his fast's focus on the plight of India's Muslims but said it was equally on behalf of the Hindu and Sikh minorities in Pakistan. It was "a process of self-purification for all."[146]

That day India's government announced its decision to pay Pakistan immediately fifty-five million rupees. The government ministers said they "shared the world-wide anxiety over the fast undertaken by the Father of the Nation. In common with him they have anxiously searched for ways and means to bury the hatchet of ill-will, prejudice and suspicion, which has poisoned the relations of India and Pakistan."[147]

Recognizing the government's decision as a "unique action," Gandhi said, "It ought to lead to an honorable settlement not only of the Kashmir question but of all the differences between the two dominions. Friendship should replace the present enmity."[148]

But he was unwilling to break the fast, thereby making clear he had not launched it simply to make the government fulfill an obligation it already had. He wanted much stronger evidence that the Hindus, Muslims, and Sikhs of Delhi had achieved a union of hearts that "not even the conflagration around them in all other parts of India or Pakistan will be strong enough to break."[149]

On January 16, the fourth day of the fast, Gandhi's life was fading. He "had been drinking no water and passing no urine. The physicians warned him that even if he survived the fast he would suffer permanent, serious injury."[150]

Because Gandhi continued to resist all who begged him to end the fast, they pushed him to say what test of a turn toward peace would satisfy him. It was then, as Pyarelal relates, "a telegram from Karachi came. Muslim refugees who had been driven out of Delhi asked whether they could now return to Delhi and reoccupy their original houses. 'That is the test,' Gandhiji remarked as soon as he had read the telegram."

Pyarelal immediately took the telegram "to all the Hindu and Sikh refugee camps in the city to explain to them what they had to do to enable Gandhiji to end his fast. By night 1,000 refugees had signed a declaration that they would welcome the Muslims to return and occupy their original homes." The refugees from Muslim violence said they would not try to occupy vacated Muslim homes. Refugees already settled in Muslims' houses said they were prepared to move out and make way for the return of their owners.[151]

Nehru and other government ministers responded in turn by welcoming homeless refugees into their official residences. Moved by Gandhi's fast, the people of Delhi were turning toward their former enemies with compassion.

The next day in Bombay, Badge again accompanied Apte

and Godse as far as the door of Savarkar, this time so the two assassination planners could "seek his final blessings," as Godse said.[152] Badge would testify in the trial for Gandhi's murder that this time, after the meeting, Savarkar walked out beside Godse. Savarkar said in parting to his disciple, "Return after being successful."[153] A few minutes later in a taxi, Godse said to Badge, "Savarkar has predicted that Gandhi's hundred years [the length of time Gandhi hoped to live; actually 125 years] are over. There is no doubt that our work will be successful."[154]

A pawn in the plot to kill Gandhi was Madanlal Pahwa, a militant young Hindu refugee from Pakistan. After fleeing his homeland during partition, Madanlal Pahwa was recruited in a refugee camp by Hindu Mahasabha organizer Vishnu Karkare, a follower of Savarkar. Karkare worked closely with Apte and Godse in leading anti-Muslim raids. Pahwa followed their orders. When Karkare joined the conspiracy to kill Gandhi, Pahwa came in with his mentor. Because Madanlal Pahwa knew how to use explosives, he was an asset to the group. And because of his symbolism as a refugee, he could serve, with arms salesman Badge, as a scapegoat.

On January 17, the fifth day of the fast, Gandhi's doctors warned in a bulletin, "In our opinion, it would be most undesirable to let the fast continue. Therefore it is our duty to tell the people to take immediate steps to produce the requisite conditions for ending the fast without delay."[155]

In response, Muslims, Hindus, and Sikhs came together in Delhi and formed processions of unity, converging on Birla House. One procession was over a mile long, numbering 100,000 participants.[156]

That night 130 members of a Central Peace Committee, representing all communities, assembled to adopt a pledge to convince Gandhi they had truly turned to peace. At the time Gandhi had fallen into a delirium. He asked to be taken to his bed when he was already in it.[157]

On the morning of January 18, the sixth day, while Peace Committee representatives were signing their pledge to Gandhi, they received word that his condition had suddenly worsened.

They rushed to Birla House. Over a hundred people crowded into Gandhi's room.[158] Packing the area around his bed, they told a revived Gandhi of the concrete steps already being taken to implement the peace pledge by Hindus, Muslims, Sikhs, and other communities. One after the other, they testified to the unity they were now committed to, begging him to give up his fast. Even representatives of the RSS and the Hindu Mahasabha, Savarkar's organizations, had come to join in the pledge and plead for Gandhi's life.

Looking around the circle of anxious faces, Gandhi said they had given him "all I asked for."[159] Nevertheless, he questioned them skeptically. Did they understand the implications of their pledge?

He said pointedly, "I take it that the RSS and the Mahasabha are also parties to the agreement. If they are participants in this agreement only for Delhi and not for other places, then the agreement is a great fraud. I know that such frauds are freely practiced in India today."[160]

If it turned out he had deceived himself in thinking they were all sincere, he was prepared to fast all over again. But for now, he wanted, above all, to go to Pakistan and seek unity there.[161]

At 12:25 p.m., January 18, Gandhi received a glass of orange juice from his Muslim ally Abdul Azad and began sipping it, breaking his final fast.[162]

He said at his prayer meeting that night:

> I embarked on the fast in the name of Truth whose familiar name is God. Without a living Truth God is nowhere. In the name of God we have indulged in lies [and] massacres of people, without caring whether they were innocent or guilty, men or women, children or infants. We have indulged in abductions, forcible conversions and we have done all this shamelessly. I am not aware if anybody has done these things in the name of Truth. With that same name on my lips I have broken the fast....
>
> ...The letter of my vow has been fulfilled beyond expectation through the great good will of all the citizens of

Delhi, including leaders of the Hindu Mahasabha and the
Rashtriya Swayamsevak Sangh.... Numerous messages
have come from Pakistan, not one of dissent. May God,
who is Truth, guide us as He visibly guided us during all
these six days.[163]

On the morning of January 20, Apte, Badge, and Badge's servant Shankar went to Birla House as a scouting party for
the assassination attempt late that afternoon. On the grounds,
Apte suddenly indicated to Badge "a stoutish gentleman dressed
up in a black suit" whom they spotted walking out of a building. "This is that Suhrawardy,"[164] Apte whispered, identifying
one of their targets. As Badge testified in the murder trial, "Apte
[repeating Savarkar] said that so far as possible both Gandhiji
and Suhrawardy should be 'finished.' He further said that, if it
was not possible to 'finish' both of them, then at least one of
them must be 'finished.'"[165]

The three men surveyed the prayer ground and the back access
to the servants' quarters (where through the trellis of a ventilator, one unseen assassin could shoot a praying Gandhi from
only four or five steps behind him,[166] while another could throw
a hand grenade, blowing up Gandhi and anyone near him).[167]

In the afternoon, the seven conspirators met in a room of
the Marina Hotel in Delhi. After accepting suggestions from
Badge and Karkare,[168] Apte finalized their instructions to murder Gandhi and his companions at his prayer meeting: Madanlal Pahwa was to explode a guncotton bomb on a rear wall to
panic the crowd. As soon as the bomb went off and confusion
erupted, Badge and Shankar would shoot Gandhi from the servants' quarters, shielded by the ventilator. Each of them would
also throw a hand grenade at Gandhi.[169]

Apte told Gopal Godse, Nathuram's younger brother, as well
as Pahwa and Karkare, to throw their remaining hand grenades
on Gandhi at the same time. Thus, even if the two shooters failed
to kill Gandhi, five assassins would be hurling hand grenades at
him (and hopefully Suhrawardy beside him).

Apte said that he and Nathuram Godse would signal the other five members of the assassination team to carry out their respective assignments at the right moments.[170]

When Badge arrived at Birla House, the prayer meeting was already beginning. Observing people at the back door to the servants' quarters, he realized it would be impossible to escape from there after shooting Gandhi. He quickly convinced Apte and Godse that, as he testified, "I would prefer to strike from the front. I would shoot from the open opposite where Mahatmaji sat."[171] He said Shankar, who followed his orders, would also attack Gandhi from the front. Apte and Godse agreed to the revised plan, perhaps thinking it would further expose Badge, making him a more likely scapegoat with Pahwa.

Badge, however, had developed cold feet. He went aside, and wrapped his and Shankar's revolvers in a towel along with their two hand grenades. He put the towel with its incriminating contents in a handbag. He stowed the handbag under the back seat of a waiting taxi. Then he rejoined Apte and Godse and went into the meeting, keeping his hands in his side pockets as if he were still carrying his weapons.[172]

Gandhi remained so weak from his fast that he had to be carried to the prayer meeting on a chair.[173] When he spoke to the gathering, his voice was feeble. The microphone was not working, so when Gandhi was finished, his co-worker, Dr. Sushila Nayyar, repeated the substance of his talk to the audience from her notes.[174]

Gandhi had said in a whisper, "I hope those who signed the peace pledge did so with God in the form of Truth as their witness." He added, "I have heard that there was a repudiation of the pledge on behalf of an official of the Hindu Mahasabha. I am sorry."[175]

He spoke of his disciples, Nehru and Patel, the two head ministers of the government. Everyone, Gandhi felt, should know that these two leaders were united in their respect for Muslims. "You should remember," Gandhi said, "that he who is an enemy of Muslims is an enemy of India."[176]

From the audience, Apte then signaled Pahwa to begin the assassination scenario. The young man obediently ignited the fuse for the guncotton charge in the back wall.

As the fuse burned down to the charge, Gandhi was drawing a parallel between the treatment of minorities in America and in India: "In America Negroes are still treated cruelly as if they were slaves, and yet the Americans indulge in tall talk about social equality. They do not realize the injustice of their actions.... We assume we are better people and cannot do such things. And yet, think of what happens here."[177]

A deafening explosion suddenly shook the prayer ground. A large chunk of the back wall collapsed. Smoke and dust rose in the air.[178] The two Godses, Apte, and Karkare waited anxiously for Badge and Shankar to launch their attack on Gandhi.

Gandhi raised his hand. He gestured to the crowd to calm down. The people returned to their places. The secretly disarmed Badge and Shankar did nothing. Witnesses pointed out Pahwa to the police. While Pahwa was being arrested, all six of his co-conspirators melted into the crowd and escaped.

Madanlal Pahwa was interrogated initially at Birla House. In response to the police's questions, he gave only one answer—that he exploded the bomb "because I did not like Gandhiji's policy of maintaining peace and friendship."[179]

That night congratulatory messages for Gandhi's escape from death poured into Birla House. Lady Mountbatten, the British viceroy's wife, rushed over to praise Gandhi for his bravery.

Gandhi said he had been ignorant, not brave. At the time he had not realized it was an attempt on his life. He thought it was just some soldiers practicing nearby with munitions.

He said, "On this occasion I have shown no bravery. If somebody fired at me point-blank and I faced his bullet with a smile, repeating the name of Rama in my heart, I should indeed be deserving of congratulations."[180]

He said no one should blame the young man who was arrested: "He had taken it for granted that I am an enemy of Hinduism. When he says he was doing the bidding of God, he is only making God an accomplice in a wicked deed. But it cannot be so.

Therefore those who are behind him or whose tool he is, should know that this sort of thing will not save Hinduism."[181]

As in Dhingra's assassination of Curzon Wyllie in 1909, Gandhi knew the real responsibility for the crime lay in the shadows—as in fact it did, in a conspiracy inspired in both cases by the same man, Vinayak Savarkar.

Gandhi was under no illusion that Pahwa's arrest meant the threat was over. When he was told a co-worker had said the explosion at the prayer meeting might turn out to have been nothing but a harmless prank, Gandhi laughed at the thought. He exclaimed, "The fool! Don't you see? There is a terrible and widespread conspiracy behind it."[182]

While his co-workers went about their business, Gandhi prepared to meet his death.

Nathuram Godse and Narayan Apte retreated to Bombay, where they succeeded in reuniting with their closest cohort, Vishnu Karkare. In the meantime, those whom Godse and Apte had left in charge of their newspaper, *Hindu Rashtra*, reported the assassination attempt as the work of anti-Gandhi refugees. *Hindu Rashtra*'s headline proclaimed: "Representative Reaction Shown by Enraged Hindu Refugees Against the Appeasement Policy of Gandhiji."[183] Fixing the blame for the murder attempt—or from the standpoint of Gandhi's enemies, the credit—on refugees was easy. The only conspirator seized by the police was refugee Madanlal Pahwa.

At a Delhi police station, Pahwa soon confessed the entire plot to his interrogators.[184] He named for the police one of the conspirators, whom he called "Kirkree" (his mentor, Karkare).[185] In describing each of his six companions, he said one of them was the editor of the Poona newspaper, *Hindu Rashtra* or *Agrani*—a definitive identification of Nathuram Godse, whom he knew under the pseudonym "Deshpande."[186] Pahwa led the police to the room in the Marina Hotel where Godse and Apte, who were registered under "S. and M. Deshpande," had held their final planning session with the others. When the police searched the room, they found in a drawer a typed press release from a Hindu Mahasabha leader, Ashutosh Lahiri, that repudiated "his organization having signed the nine-point pledge required by Gandhiji."[187] The press release said the Hindu Mahasabha was "opposed to the basic policy of Mahatma Gandhi and his followers in regard to the treatment meted out to Muslim minorities in India."[188] Here was an important clue that Pahwa's co-conspirators were linked with the Hindu Mahasabha. Laundry that the room's occupants had given to the hotel for washing included three items bearing the initials "NVG" (standing for "Nathuram Vinayak Godse").

The importance of all this evidence identifying Gandhi's would-be assassins was underlined by a chilling statement Madanlal Pahwa made to the police: "They will come again."[189] Nathuram Godse, in the company of Apte and Karkare, would fulfill Pahwa's prophecy to the police by shooting Gandhi to death on January 30.

How was that to happen?

Incriminating, identifying information was in the hands of the police. Pahwa was warning them that the killers would return.

Moreover, Madanlal Pahwa had already divulged the plot to kill Gandhi the week before the conspirators even tried to carry it out. He had told his employer in Bombay, Professor J. C. Jain, about his upcoming role, "throwing a bomb" as a diversion at Gandhi's prayer meeting, so that his associates could kill Gandhi.[190] Jain thought Pahwa was just making up the story, until he was shocked to read a January 21 newspaper article about Pahwa's arrest for the bombing incident. Jain then managed to meet with B. G. Kher, premier of the province of Bombay, and Morarji Desai, home minister of the province of Bombay. He had succeeded in gaining the attention of the two most important government officials in Bombay on the urgent matter of Gandhi's impending assassination, over a week before it would happen. Jain informed the government leaders that he knew from Pahwa that the bombing was part of what "appeared to be a big conspiracy" to kill Gandhi: "Madanlal had told me that [the conspirators] had formed a party, which was financed by one Karkare from Ahmednagar," who had visited him along with Pahwa.[191] A further connection was Savarkar, who Pahwa said had met with him for two hours, praising the young Hindu refugee for exploits such as his attempt to dynamite the house of a Muslim.[192]

On hearing Jain's story, Home Minister Desai had, he said later, "a strong feeling that Savarkar was behind the conspiracy."[193] Desai said he passed on Jain's information that night to his deputy police commissioner, J. D. Nagarvala, ordering him, first, "to arrest Karkare" (Karkare had an outstanding warrant for his arrest in another case but had not yet been found), second, "to keep a close watch on Savarkar's house and his movements," and third, "to find out as to who were the persons involved in the plot."[194] Desai said he also shared Jain's information on the plot the next day, January 22, 1948, in Ahmedabad, with the Indian Union government's home minister, Vallabhbhai Patel, who was in charge of the national government's security apparatus.[195]

Following the bombing incident and Pahwa's arrest, Patel wanted to increase Gandhi's security. He told Gandhi he "wanted the police to search every person coming to his prayer meetings."[196] As Patel must have known Gandhi would do, the mahatma absolutely refused to allow a police search as a condition for a person's admittance to prayer. "My faith," he said, "does not allow me to put myself under any kind of human protection at the prayer time, when I have put myself under the sole protection of God."[197] According to Pyarelal, Patel, finding Gandhi adamant, "resigned himself to whatever Providence might have in store."[198]

The home minister's apparent resignation to providence, in what would turn out to be a time when Gandhi's assassins were regrouping, did not go unchallenged after the assassination. On February 6, 1948, in a special session of the Indian Parliament on Gandhi's murder, Member of Parliament Rohini Kumar Chaudhury raised a critical question to Patel: "Can I ask if the police seek the convenience of the person they are assigned to protect? The truth is that in the matter of security the convenience of neither the governor nor the governor general is asked."

Patel answered: "As far as the issue pertaining to the current matter, the concerned person was of a different category, and in his case it was impossible for the police to act without seeking his advice."[199]

Patel was right that the police had to consult Gandhi on such an intrusive matter as body searches. However, Patel's responsibility for Gandhi's safety did not end with the mahatma's predictable rejection of searches. Patel had in fact increased the security at Birla House after the bomb explosion on the 20th, multiplying the number of police officers.[200] He did so with Gandhi's approval.

When asked by a co-worker about the increase in security, Gandhi said, "I'm not worried as you people are. If I had disallowed the posting of a guard, I should have added to the many worries of Sardar [Patel] and Jawahar [Nehru] one more worry about my safety. Their responsibility is already very heavy."[201]

Gandhi insisted Rama continued to be his only real protector, but gave his express consent to reasonable security measures (short of searching people) that Patel and Nehru might feel were necessary for his safety. He said it was up to them: "They only believe that this police guard will save my life. Hence let them do whatever they like."[202]

Pyarelal told the Kapur Commission that, apart from the added officers, he "could not say whether any special [police] precautions were taken after the bomb was thrown." However, he was certain of one thing: "Mahatma would have been protected if the police had arrested those persons about whom indications had been given in Madanlal's statement."[203]

Why didn't the police carry out such obvious arrests?

As of January 21, both the Delhi police and the Bombay police had in their possession statements identifying key members of the ongoing conspiracy to kill Gandhi. Moreover, they were in touch with one another.[204] Yet for nine days the assassins moved about freely, until three of them, Apte, Godse, and Karkare, returned on the 30th to another prayer meeting in Delhi, where Godse then killed Gandhi.

For that to happen, without any intervening arrests to prevent the assassination, strange events had to occur. And they did.

On January 21, Delhi's inspector general of police, T. G. Sanjevi, sent two of his officers to Bombay to brief the Bombay deputy police commissioner, J. D. Nagarvala, on Pahwa's confession. The Delhi officers claimed that when they saw the Bombay commissioner, Nagarvala, on the next two days, he met with them only perfunctorily. In return, they simply gave him an English note on the case (which Nagarvala denied receiving). They did "not orally tell Mr. Nagarvala what was within their knowledge," including Pahwa's naming Karkare as a co-conspirator or Pahwa's identification of the editor of the Poona newspaper, the *Hindu Rashtra* or *Agrani*, as another co-conspirator. The officers told the commissioner nothing they knew that would identify the assassins.[205] Nor did Nagarvala share with them the contents of the statement he already had from Professor Jain that also identified Pahwa, Karkare, as well as their association with Savarkar—"all pointers to attempted political assassination by Savarkar's followers."[206] Each police contingent acted as if they were obliged not to speak in a meaningful way, each claiming later that noncooperation by the other was to blame for Gandhi's death. Nagarvala told the two visiting officers that he had the investigation under control and ordered them to return to Delhi.[207]

In the meantime, Nagarvala's Bombay police, following Morarji Desai's orders, were keeping what proved to be an ineffective watch on Savarkar's home. Nagarvala "stated in his Crime Report No. 1 that Savarkar was at the back of the conspiracy and that he was feigning illness and was wrongly giving out that he was out of politics."[208]

At this point Gandhi had just seven days left before his assassins would return.

When the Delhi police officers returned from Bombay, having achieved nothing, *The Kapur Report* noted that they "should have at once telephoned or telegraphed to the Poona police, giving them information about the editor of the *Agrani* and inquiring as to who he was, who his companions were, what his activities were and what his haunts were, and should have made a requisition for their arrest."[209] All they did was submit a report on their unsuccessful trip to Bombay.

Gandhi had five days left to live.

Also on January 25, Delhi's inspector general Sanjevi met with Bombay's deputy inspector general, U. H. Rana, who happened to be in Delhi. Sanjevi gave Rana a copy of Pahwa's most recent, January 24 statement to the Delhi police, to hand over personally to the Bombay police. Pahwa had by this time mentioned not only the editor of the *Hindu Rashtra* (Godse) but also its "proprietor" or publisher (Apte) as his co-conspirators.[210]

Rana departed for Bombay on a mission that was late but could still have saved Gandhi's life. However, he decided to go by train instead of air. He said later it was "because he did not like flying."[211] He also chose a very long train route to Bombay, taking him across half of India on a thirty-six-hour train ride.[212] During this time, Godse and Apte were actually in Bombay, consulting with Savarkar and renewing their attempt to kill Gandhi.[213]

When Rana finally arrived in Bombay on January 27, Godse and Apte had just left by plane for Delhi. Gandhi had three days left. Rana then met with Commissioner Nagarvala. Rana said he showed the "full statement of Madanlal to Mr. Nagarvala, but took it back from him and Mr. Nagarvala did not read it through."[214] *The Kapur Report* observed that Nagarvala "did not ask Mr. Rana as to the contents of the statement of Madanlal because Mr. Rana appeared to be satisfied with what he (Nagarvala) had already done. This is rather a peculiar statement because Mr. Nagarvala was working out the information given by Professor Jain, which had been conveyed to him by Mr. Morarji Desai, and Madanlal's statement at Delhi would have been helpful in working out the information."[215]

Why did Rana not give Nagarvala the statement, providing further information on Pahwa's co-conspirators in the plot to kill Gandhi?

And why did Nagarvala not retain or copy the statement, or at the very least read it through?

When it came to identifying the editor and proprietor of the *Hindu Rashtra*, the ignorance and disinterest of the various police officials became even more puzzling. The Kapur Commission discovered that the Indian government had this information in its files in Delhi all along. Copies of the "Annual Statement of Newspapers" had been sent to both the Home Department and the Information and Broadcasting Department of the Government of India. The newspaper list named N. V. Godse as the editor, and N. D. Apte as the proprietor, of the *Hindu Rashtra,* described by the document as "a Savarkarite group paper."[216]

Inspector General T. G. Sanjevi was also the director of the Intelligence Bureau, the highest police job in India.[217] For the ten days from Pahwa's capture to Gandhi's assassination, the list that identified Godse and Apte with the *Hindu Rashtra* was only a few steps away from Sanjevi in his own files. He never took those steps. Nor did any other police official.

The Kapur Report commented: "It would be unbelievable if that thing did not happen as it did, that Mr. U. H. Rana should have gone through the statement of Madanlal along with Mr. Sanjevi, as Mr. Sanjevi's note shows, and neither of them should, on the 25th January, have taken the slightest trouble to find out from the Intelligence Bureau or the Press Information Bureau" who the proprietor (or editor) of the *Hindu Rashtra* was.[218]

And so it went, in a police investigation marked by lethargy, delays, and official indifference toward tracking and arresting the men who were stalking Gandhi. Pahwa said they would come back, and they did. The police by their inaction gave the assassins another chance.

Why?

The veil was lifted for a moment when Nagarvala was asked why he did not arrest Savarkar or detain him. "His reply was that he could not do so before the murder as that would not only have caused commotion in the Maharashtrian region but an upheaval."[219]

Nagarvala was admitting that before Gandhi's assassination,

he saw Savarkar and his followers as too powerful to be stopped. From a police standpoint, allowing Gandhi's assassins to move about freely until they killed him was a concession to power.

On the evening of January 27, Gandhi met with Vincent Sheean, an American journalist who had come all the way from a farmhouse in Vermont with a burning need to see him. Sheean had been haunted by a fear Gandhi would soon be killed. He was driven by a terrible sense that Gandhi's assassination would occur before Sheean could pose critical questions to him that had arisen from the Second World War and the atomic bomb.[220] How had a war that needed to be waged against Hitler resulted in the invention of world-destructive weapons? How could humanity survive its own creations?

Sheean was deeply relieved when Pyarelal ushered him in to meet the still-living Gandhi after his prayer meeting. The tall reporter and the short *satyagrahi* paced the room's carpet side by side, as Sheean fired questions at the mahatma. He started philosophically but was brought down to earth quickly by Gandhi.

"I propose to begin," Sheean said, "with action and the fruits of action."

Gandhi stopped walking. He needed to make a point. He looked up at Sheean with a birdlike motion.

"Let me get one thing clear," he said. "I have typhoid fever. Doctors are sent for and by means of injections of sulpha drugs or something of the kind they save my life. This, however, proves nothing. It might be that it would be more valuable to humanity for me to die."

Gandhi gazed up at Sheean. He waited for the point that it might be more valuable to humanity for him to die to sink in.

"Is that quite clear?" he asked. "If it is not, I will repeat it."

"No, sir," said Sheean. "I think I understand it."

The two men resumed walking.

"How can a righteous battle produce a catastrophic result?" asked Sheean. He was thinking especially of World War II.

"Because of the means used," Gandhi said. "Means are not to be distinguished from ends." Gandhi had been challenged on this insight by Savarkar, during their conflict in London over the question of using assassinations, as Savarkar's group was doing, to achieve national liberation. Impossible, said Gandhi to Savarkar and his student militants. Now Gandhi was explaining the coherence of means and ends all over again to Sheean, three days before Gandhi would be assassinated by a more recent follower of Savarkar. Gandhi said, "If violent means are used, there will be a bad result."

"Is this true at all times and places?" Sheean asked.

"*I* say so," Gandhi said. "The terms are convertible. No good act can produce an evil result. Evil means, even for a good end, produce evil results."[221]

Sheean would not let go: "I was thinking of our war [against Hitler], which in my view was a righteous battle. I knew some of the leaders on our side."

Gandhi nodded, which Sheean took to mean Gandhi's agreement that both Roosevelt and Churchill had been righteous in intention.

Sheean continued: "How can such a truly righteous battle as our fight against the evil of fascism produce the result which now faces us?"

Gandhi leaned toward Sheean. He said gently with great sadness, "Your ends may have been good but your means were bad. That is not the way of truth."

"Those who govern us," Sheean said, "are obviously concerned with the fruits of action rather than with the truth of action. How, then, are we to be well governed?"

"You must give up the worship of mammon," Gandhi said. Sheean knew Gandhi meant Americans had to stop worshiping mammon. Gandhi outlined for Sheean a vision of representative democracy, in which those who were corrupted could be recalled from office by those who were not. He paused, then added, "Have nothing to do with power."

"Do you mean that power corrupts?" asked Sheean.

"Yes," Gandhi said, "I am afraid I do mean that power corrupts." Yet, as Gandhi knew, he was not going to give up counseling people corrupted by power, including his own disciples in the Indian government. He meant he would never seek power himself. Nor should anyone seek political power who was experimenting in the ultimate force of truth through nonviolence. Gandhi was committed to realizing a more profound kind of force—truth-force, seeing God face to face in the poorest human beings he encountered, and drawing power through them. A further step was to see God face to face even in those who planned to kill him (Savarkar) and who did (Godse), yet drawing love through them, as in his mutual bow with his assassin at the moment of his death.[222]

"Nonviolence," Gandhi said, "is absolutely necessary for a good result."[223]

Gandhi told Sheean at the end of their meeting that he would welcome seeing him again: "And consider that a standing invitation!"[224] Then, as Sheean notes, Gandhi "added very gently, in a voice that would have melted the heart of an enemy (and I was no enemy): 'If there is no time, will you understand?'"[225]

The reporter wrote on his return to the United States after Gandhi's assassination: "He knew that I had come across half the world in a state approaching despair to ask him to tell me the truth—this much he knew within a few minutes, by intuition—and he set out to do so without regard for the consequences. What I had encountered, quite beyond expectation or probability, was a manifestation of divine pity."[226]

On January 29, Vincent Sheean accompanied Jawaharlal Nehru to a mass meeting in Amritsar, near India's northwest border with Pakistan. Four hundred thousand people gathered in a park to hear their country's prime minister. Sheean from his spot near Nehru was awed by the sea of humanity. He was also struck by what Nehru said in "a speech of great political importance. It was the first time any member of the government of India had openly attacked the Hindu reactionary or proto-fascist organizations by name—those organizations which were, within twenty-four hours, to take the life of Mahatma Gandhi."[227]

As a border city, Amritsar was filled with Hindu and Sikh refugees from Pakistan. Nehru's audience included a large number of people seething with revenge against Muslims, whom they blamed for their plight. They were being egged on by the Hindu Mahasabha and RSS organizations that Nehru identified and attacked, on the eve of Gandhi's murder.

Nehru's speech was courageous, given at a critical juncture of history. Unfortunately, almost no one in the vast crowd heard it. In a strange turn of events, as Sheean witnessed, "the loudspeaker apparatus failed and not a word of Mr. Nehru's speech could be heard."[228]

On the same day, in a letter to a friend, Gandhi wrote that his mission in Delhi was not quite over: "If I could be said to have 'done' in Delhi, it might not be necessary for me to be here to keep my pledge (of 'do or die'). But that is for the people here to judge. The question will perhaps be decided tomorrow."[229]

Just before Gandhi fell asleep that final night, in a conversation with one of his attendants, he said once again that if he was "the man of God that I claimed to be," he would have to respond to his assassin by breathing God's name: "If someone were to end my life by putting a bullet through me—as someone tried to do with a bomb the other day—and I met his bullet without a groan, and breathed my last taking God's name, then alone would I have made good my claim."[230]

On Friday, January 30, Gandhi's last day on earth, Pyarelal reported back to him the response of the Hindu Mahasabha president, Dr. Shyama Prasad Mookerjee, to a concern Gandhi had raised. Dr. Mookerjee, as the formal head of Savarkar's organization, was a minister in Nehru's cabinet—a sign of the power that the forces the prime minister denounced in his unheard speech the night before had gained in his own government. Gandhi had asked Mookerjee if he would please use his authority, as the Mahasabha leader, to put a curb on the activities of a Mahasabha worker "who had been delivering highly inflammatory speeches containing incitement to assassination of some Congress leaders."[231]

Pyarelal told Gandhi Dr. Mookerjee's "halting and unsatisfactory reply. It seems he had underestimated the seriousness of the danger represented by such irresponsible utterances and activities and the heavy toll they would exact before long."

Pyarelal observes in his biography: "Gandhiji's brow darkened as I repeated to him Dr. Mookerjee's reply."[232]

During his final morning, Gandhi encouraged Pyarelal in his experiments in constructive nonviolence in the still-troubled region of Noakhali. Gandhi said, "How I have longed to do all these things myself! What we need is to shed the fear of death and steal into the hearts and affections of those we serve.... If there is nothing but love in the heart, your words will go home."[233]

At 4:00 p.m., Gandhi engaged in an intense discussion with Patel, who was on the verge of resigning as home minister because of his deepening conflicts with Nehru. Gandhi considered both men indispensable to the government. He counseled reconciliation. His death would accomplish it. That evening, after Gandhi's assassination, Nehru would lie sobbing with his head in the lap of Patel, near their master's dead body. Gandhi's two prodigal sons, who had betrayed him by conceding partition, knew he had never stopped loving them. The two leaders, reconciled by Gandhi's martyrdom, would continue to rule India together until Patel's death in December 1950.

When Gandhi finally broke away from counseling Patel at 5:10, he was told that leaders from the Indian peninsula of Kathiawar were outside requesting an appointment with him.

"Tell them to come after prayer," he said. "I shall see them—if I am alive."[234]

As Gandhi finished walking across the grass to the prayer ground, he was silent. With his hands resting on the shoulders of his grandnieces, Abha and Manu, he ascended the six brick steps to the terrace that was his prayer site. Manu has described the next moments.

"Then, lifting his hands off our shoulders, he folded them to greet the assembled people, and walked on. I was walking on his right. From the same direction a stout young man in khaki dress, with his hands folded, pushed his way through the crowd and came near us."[235]

The man in khaki was Nathuram Godse. As Manu tried to brush past him, saying, "Bapu is already ten minutes late," Godse shoved her out of the way. Manu bent down to pick up the rosary she had dropped.[236] Godse was bowing to Gandhi. Raising his head, he pulled out an automatic pistol and fired three quick shots, one into Gandhi's stomach and two into his chest. As Gandhi fell, blessing his assassin, his last words were "Rama! Rama!"[237]

Vincent Sheean was ten feet away. He had been given another appointment to interview Gandhi that evening, following the prayer meeting. Sheean had been watching Gandhi walk through the grass to the prayer ground. As the small figure began to climb the steps, the reporter's view of him was blocked by the crowd.

When Sheean heard three small explosions, he said in horror to a friend standing beside him, "What's that?" As his friend grew pale, Sheean knew his anticipation of Gandhi's murder had come true. He recoiled against a brick wall and felt in his head "a wavelike disturbance [like] a storm at sea—wind and wave surging tremendously back and forth.... *How can such things be?*"[238] For days the question kept streaming through his mind.

He had already forgotten Gandhi's statement and question to him: "It might be that it would be more valuable to humanity for me to die. Is that quite clear? If it is not, I will repeat it."

Sheean had said, "No, sir. I think I understand it." But he had not. Because of his affection for his teacher, Gandhi, and his desire to learn more from him face to face, now in the wake of his assassination Sheean could not accept Gandhi's first point in their dialogue—that it might be more valuable to humanity for him to die.

The impact of Gandhi's death has been described by Dennis Dalton:

> Gandhi's assassination, more than any other single event, served to stop the communal violence surrounding partition. It achieved this in the same way as his fasts, by causing people to pause and reflect in the midst of their fear, anger, and enmity: to ask themselves if the cost was worth it. A mixture of motives was probably at work, merciful and rational as well as grief-stricken or guilt-ridden. But somehow a determination came to stop the killing.... There was no higher tribute to his life than the impact of his death, his final statement for swaraj.[239]

Judge Atma Charan, the presiding judge in the trial for Gandhi's murder, delivered a damning judgment concerning the police's role in abetting the assassination. He said at the trial's conclusion:

> I may bring to the notice of the Central Government the slackness of the police in the investigation of the case during the period between January 20, 1948, and January 30, 1948. The Delhi Police had obtained a detailed statement from Madanlal K. Pahwa soon after his arrest on January 20, 1948. The Bombay Police had also been reported the statement of Dr. J. C. Jain that he had made to the Honorable Mr. Morarji Desai on January 21, 1948. The Delhi Police and the Bombay police had contacted each other soon after these two statements had been made. Yet the police miserably failed to derive any advantage from these two statements. Had the slightest keenness been shown in the investigation of the case at that stage the tragedy probably could have been avoided.[240]

Gandhi's great grandson, Tushar Gandhi, has written about police complicity in the assassination:

> According to a secret report submitted to Home Minister Sardar Patel, many in the police force and many bureau-

crats were secret members of the RSS and the Hindu Mahasabha, and were actively supporting and promoting the ideology of the Hindu extremist organizations.... The measures taken by the police between 20th and 30th January 1948 were more to ensure the smooth progress of the murderers, than to try and prevent [Gandhi's] murder....

In hindsight it can only be said that, in Gandhi's murder, the police by their negligence and inactions were as much guilty as the murderers themselves.[241]

To what degree were the government's leaders also responsible for Gandhi's death?

The official in charge of security for Prime Minister Nehru, G. K. Handoo, explained later to the Kapur Commission in its investigation of Gandhi's assassination what should have been done to protect him from his assassins. Handoo said the government had a security blueprint to follow in such matters.[242]

Given the identification of the conspirators provided by Pahwa and Jain after the bomb explosion, Handoo said that Bombay and Poona police officers (with their familiarity of Godse, Apte, and other co-conspirators) should have been enlisted as spotters. They should have been posted to watch for the assassins at the Delhi airport, railway stations, hotels, and other key Delhi locations, particularly at Birla House during the prayer meetings. Two rings of plainclothes security police should have been formed to protect Gandhi, the first ring two to three yards from him, and the second ring twenty-five yards away.[243]

These were the kind of standard government security measures carried out for the prime minister and other VIPs, especially in the context of a recognized threat. Gandhi, considered "the father of the nation," more than qualified for such security during the period of January 20-30, 1948, when a co-conspirator in custody had said repeatedly that Gandhi's assassins would return. As MP questioner Rohini Chaudhury pointed out to Patel, Gandhi's consent to security (except in the case of body searches) was not required. Nor was Gandhi adamantly opposed to a police presence. He had agreed, in deference to Nehru's and Patel's burden of responsibility, to whatever measures they thought necessary for his security (short of body searches). "Let them do whatever they like," he had said.[244]

Yet, in the ten days between the bombing and Gandhi's murder, no such standard security measures were taken to protect him. Nehru and Patel did not deploy their security police as they would have done normally in such a situation—as was in fact done for themselves immediately after Gandhi's murder, out of concern for their own lives. At a critical time, under a clearly identified threat, they failed to protect the life of the man they, their country, and the world most revered.

Savarkar was among those charged with Gandhi's murder. Digambar Badge, who turned state's evidence, testified in the murder trial about Godse's and Apte's meetings with Savarkar. Savarkar, however, was found not guilty because of a lack of corroborative evidence. Godse and Apte protected Savarkar all the way to their executions, denying vehemently any connection with Savarkar in the conspiracy.

Savarkar read a fifty-seven-page statement in his defense. In it he told the story of his life, portraying himself as a self-sacrificing patriot. He flatly denied all the charges against him. In conclusion, he cited statements he had made that he claimed showed his admiration and affection for Gandhi.

P. L. Inamdar, a defense lawyer who professed a great admiration for Savarkar, was taken aback by Savarkar's performance in defense of himself: "[Savarkar] read out the statement in the Court with all the gimmicks of an orator bemoaning his fate of being charged with the murder of Mahatmaji by the independent Indian government, when he had admired and eulogized the personality of the Mahatmaji so sincerely and so often. Savarkar actually wiped his cheeks in court while reading this part of his oration."[245]

Although Savarkar was seated next to Godse in the defendants' dock, he totally ignored him and the other defendants. Savarkar knew it was to his legal advantage if he acted as if he bore no relation to his co-defendants, especially the confessed shooter of Gandhi. Godse told friends how he "yearned for a touch of [Savarkar's] hand, a word of sympathy, or at least a look of compassion."[246] Godse, the triggerman, maintained his loyalty to Savarkar to the gallows, proclaiming his mentor's innocence to the end. While Godse in his courtroom speech of defense derided the prosecutor because he "painted me as a mere tool in the hands of Veer Savarkar,"[247] his teacher sat impassively, according to defense counsel Inamdar, like "a sphinx sculpted in stone."[248]

Yet critics have maintained that Savarkar, in spite of his self-defensive, public coldness toward Godse, was actually the composer of Godse's surprisingly eloquent, written statement. It took Godse nine hours to deliver his courtroom speech.[249] Tushar Gandhi observed:

> The language of the statement leads one to the conclusion that much of it either flows directly from the pen of the master orator and wizard wordsmith, V. D. Savarkar, or was definitely embellished by him. Savarkar possessed a magical command over the spoken and written word. Even if not entirely written by Savarkar, the final draft was surely worked on by him converting it into a highly emotionally charged document.... It was known that the accused were free to confer with each other in prison, and on several occasions guards had been caught smuggling out messages from the accused. There is no reason to believe that Nathuram was not able to get his mentor and guru, V. D. Savarkar, to help him polish what is today referred to by Nathuram's ideological offspring as his last will and testament.[250]

The fact that Judge Atma Charan allowed Nathuram Godse, Gandhi's confessed assassin, to speak for nine hours, in an ideological assault on Gandhi and a judicial defense of Savarkar, shows just how much the court was subservient to the political power of Gandhi's murderers. Godse's speech condemned his murder victim for his "submission to the Muslims' blows."[251] Godse claimed he had to kill Gandhi for surrendering India to the Muslims, lest he "lead the nation to ruin and make it easy for Pakistan to enter the remaining India and occupy the same."[252] Gandhi's "teachings of absolute 'Ahimsa,'" Godse said, "would ultimately result in the emasculation of the Hindu community and thus make the community incapable of resisting the aggression or inroads of other communities especially the Muslims."[253] Godse contrasted Gandhi's teaching of nonviolence with the militant Hindu ideology of "Brave" Savarkar, "the ablest and most faithful advocate of [the] Hindu cause."[254] Godse, however, insisted repeatedly that Savarkar had nothing to do with Gandhi's murder.

Why did the judge give Godse a courtroom platform from which he could launch an extended attack on the reputation of the man he had already shot to death? When Godse, and in effect, Savarkar, were allowed to attack Gandhi in a nine-hour courtroom diatribe, the defendants became the prosecution. It was a clear prelude to Savarkar being declared not guilty by the judge.[255]

It was only after Savarkar's death in 1966 that a government commission reviewing Gandhi's assassination revealed that the corroborative evidence to convict Savarkar had been in the government's possession all along. On March 4, 1948, three months before the Gandhi murder trial began, Savarkar's bodyguard, Appa Ramchandra Kasar, and his secretary, Gajanan Vishnu Damle, gave recorded statements to the Bombay police confirming that meetings between Savarkar, Godse, and Apte had in fact taken place before the assassination. Kasar and Damle also revealed that Savarkar had additional meetings in January with his other indicted co-conspirators Karkare, Pahwa, Badge, and Parchure.[256]

Justice J. L. Kapur, who chaired the commission on Gandhi's murder, observed in his 1970 report:

> All this shows that people who were subsequently involved in the murder of Mahatma Gandhi were all congregating sometime or the other at Savarkar Sadan and sometimes

had long interviews with Savarkar. It is significant that Karkare and Madanlal [Pahwa] visited Savarkar before they left for Delhi and Apte and Godse visited him both before the bomb was thrown and also before the murder was committed and on each occasion they had long interviews.[257]

Bombay Police Commissioner Nagarvala, who acted with so little urgency while Gandhi was still alive, stated in a letter on January 31, 1948, that in the wake of Gandhi's assassination, he had arrested Kasar, Savarkar's bodyguard, and Damle, his secretary. Nagarvala learned from them that Godse and Apte had met with Savarkar for forty minutes "on the eve of their departure to Delhi"[258]—a critical meeting in addition to those identified by Badge. Kasar and Damle "had admitted that these two [Godse and Apte] had access to the house of Savarkar without any restriction."[259]

When summarizing evidence tying Savarkar into the plot, Justice Kapur stated in his report: "All these facts taken together were destructive of any theory other than the conspiracy to murder [Gandhi] by Savarkar and his group."[260]

Home Minister Patel and Prime Minister Nehru soon learned that Savarkar was behind Gandhi's murder. Less than a month after the assassination, Patel wrote to Nehru: "It was a fanatical wing of the Hindu Mahasabha directly under Savarkar that [hatched] the conspiracy and saw it through."[261]

Yet government prosecutors never called to the murder trial's witness stand either Savarkar's bodyguard, Kasar, or his secretary, Damle. Their statements would have corroborated and added to Badge's testimony regarding Savarkar's meetings with Godse and Apte. Neither did the prosecution cite from the interviews Kasar and Damle had given the police on the Savarkar-Godse-Apte meetings. The prosecution ignored these two key witnesses and their recorded information. Their testimony would have closed the government's conspiracy case against Savarkar.[262]

So why did the government hold back critical evidence that would have convicted Savarkar?

A revealing exchange occurred in the Gandhi murder trial, when witness Morarji Desai, the Bombay government's home minister, was cross-examined by Savarkar's lawyer. Desai was testifying on what Professor Jain had told him, after Pahwa's arrest for the January 20 attempt to kill Gandhi: Pahwa told Jain earlier that Savarkar was involved in the plot. Desai said he then ordered the police to place a watch on Savarkar's house.[263] Savarkar's attorney asked Desai: "Did you have any other information about Savarkar, besides Professor Jain's statement, for directing steps to be taken as regards him?"

Desai responded: "Shall I give the full facts? I am prepared to answer. It is for him [Savarkar] to decide."[264]

Savarkar's defender withdrew the question. He asked the judge to delete the exchange from the record as well as his motion to delete. The judge complied. The record was sanitized.[265]

Why did Morarji Desai, a prominent official who would eventually become India's prime minister, defer to the defendant, Savarkar, rather than simply "give the full facts" about the further evidence Desai had on Savarkar?

Why was it "for him [Savarkar, the defendant] to decide" what Desai, the government officer in charge, was prepared but reluctant to testify?

This courtroom encounter, deleted from the trial record but reported by a *Times of India* journalist in attendance,[266] suggests the unspeakable power that Savarkar retained even as Gandhi's charged assassin. The looming possibility that Savarkar would be convicted on the evidence threatened the government prosecuting him. It was for Savarkar to decide what Desai should say on the witness stand.

Tushar Gandhi, citing Patel, concluded that Savarkar was acquitted because of an unspeakable political necessity: "Patel had admitted that the government had 'annoyed the Muslims, [and] we could not afford to anger the Hindus too.' If Savarkar had been found guilty and sentenced, it would have caused a massive Hindu extremist reaction, which the Congress was scared of facing."[267]

Savarkar composed his last book, as his publisher notes, "during his illness and old age"[268] in the 1960s. In that summary work, *Six Glorious Epochs of Indian History*, Savarkar tried to justify the murder of Gandhi in an oblique way. According to his epochal reading of Indian history, it was periodically necessary to assassinate weak Indian leaders to build up the national forces that could repel foreign invaders.

In the first of his "glorious epochs" of national liberation, Savarkar described how in 321 B.C. the rebel prince, Chandragupta, and his advisor, Chanakya, "had to assassinate, as an unavoidable national duty," the reigning emperor, Samrat Mahapadma Nanda, "who had proved himself thoroughly incapable of repulsing" the Greek invasion of Alexander the Great.[269] The weak emperor's assassination was a national mandate.

In Savarkar's second "glorious epoch," in 184 B.C., a traitorous general, Pushyamitra, "had to cut off the head of Brihadrath Maurya," the Buddhist emperor, "simply as a national duty."[270] Savarkar claimed assassination was again a national imperative, in this case against an emperor whose pacifist, Buddhist beliefs had made him "vacillating and weak."[271]

What Savarkar claims as a truth of ancient Indian history carries the implied argument that it was equally a national duty for him and his followers to assassinate Gandhi. Because Gandhi was a major obstacle to Savarkar's vision of a militarized, exclusively Hindu nation, Gandhi, too, had to be killed.[272] Savarkar is careful not to make explicit so bold a claim, which would renew suspicions about his own role in the murder. His analogy between the two emperors and Gandhi is also a stretch. Gandhi was no emperor, and his massive *satyagraha* campaigns were not examples of weakness. They freed India and brought down the British Empire.

From the time of their London conflicts over Lord Wyllie's assassination, Gandhi and Savarkar differed radically in their interpretation of *The Ramayana*. For Savarkar, Rama as the incarnation of good had to kill evil literally in the form of Ravana, the embodiment of evil. Because Gandhi's *satyagraha* (truth-force) movement was, Savarkar claimed, another threat to make India weak, he condemned it as an evil force. The *satyagraha* movement was based, he told his prison mates in 1921, on "the perverse doctrine of nonviolence and truth,"[273] as articulated by Gandhi. In a contradictory analysis, Savarkar thought the Gandhian illusion of nonviolence and truth was achieving so powerful a hold over the people that "it was bound to destroy the power of the country." Savarkar condemned the nonviolent movement without reservation as evil: "It is an illusion, a hallucination, not unlike the hurricane that sweeps over a land only to destroy it. It is a disease of insanity, an epidemic and megalomania."[274]

So it was, that on his release from prison, Savarkar predicted to his fellow prisoners his own reenactment of Rama's victory over evil by killing Ravana, "some day, sometime," which "must give you acute pain."[275] Savarkar believed there was one effective way to destroy the evil of nonviolence that would otherwise weaken and destroy India. Rama had to finish Ravana and win the battle. Rama, as embodied by Savarkar and the hands of his followers, had to kill Ravana, as embodied by Gandhi.

Gandhi drew a nonviolent lesson from the symbolic story. Rama as the good had to resist nonviolently the evil of violence in order to overcome it. The final death of Ravana was symbolic of an internal death in one's self. The means of redemption was to suffer violence out of love for the opponent, not kill him.

Moreover, Rama, or God, could not be seen as identical with the *satyagraha* movement, any more than Ravana, or evil, could be seen as one with the British government or the Hindu Mahasabha. Gandhi's focus was on the humanity of his opponents, which he equated with the presence of God. Truth was God, and the opponent always represented a part of the truth. Our discovering—really seeing for the first time—the truth of our opponent was the nonviolent process of redeeming evil. It was the process of being redeemed in grace from our own partisan vision of God. Rama as the good, and Ravana as the evil, were present in everyone. That meant nonviolence was the way to realize our opponent's truth—the surprising process of seeing truth through our enemy's eyes, and thus through our own in a more integral way. Rama had to suffer the violent challenge of Ravana, to the point of death and transformation, to realize the unified truth of God.

Gandhi believed we had to die to our violence, not try to kill it falsely in someone else, for the redemptive power of truth and love to transform us. For that loving power of Rama to be with him to the end was his constant prayer.

On the other hand, Savarkar's purpose through his followers was not simply to kill Gandhi. It was, above all, to destroy his vision. Like the Buddha's, Gandhi's vision was a powerful, nonviolent alternative to Hindu militance. A truly successful assassination had to destroy a vision that was more inspiring than Savarkar's. Because of the very power of *satyagraha,* which could transform India into a nonviolent catalyst in the world, Savarkar and his followers thought it had to be destroyed.

Yet Savarkar was shrewd enough to know he couldn't attack Gandhi's vision head on, any more than he could attack Gandhi himself head on. Savarkar didn't have the popular strength of Gandhi, as was apparent in Gandhi's rise in power since the days of their encounters in London and Savarkar's decline. Savarkar knew he was no match for Gandhi's embodiment of the suffering of the Indian masses, any more than Hindutva was a match for *satyagraha.* So he couldn't directly attack the power of Gandhi's vision. He could only hope to cover it up, just as he strove to cover up his role in Gandhi's assassination. For that, propaganda was necessary.

Savarkar was a master assassin and propagandist, as he had shown four decades earlier in London. After his follower Madan-lal Dhingra carried out his command by murdering Curzon Wyllie, Savarkar wrote "Dhingra's" posthumously published statement. It inspired anti-British sentiments at the same time as it shielded Savarkar from blame in killing Wyllie.

He accomplished the same kind of feat in Gandhi's murder and the conspirators' trial. After inspiring and manipulating Gandhi's assassination from behind the scenes, Savarkar shunned his disciples in the courtroom, defended himself as an admirer of Gandhi, and was declared not guilty of all the charges against him. Nathuram Godse delivered an eloquent courtroom attack against the murder victim, Gandhi, that was inspired by Savarkar and probably written by him. Then Godse and Apte went loyally to their deaths, denying their master's involvement in the conspiracy. Savarkar returned to his home in Bombay and lived another seventeen years.

As Patel and Nehru should have learned from Gandhi's insistence that the truth is always paramount, their government's unwillingness to pursue the truth in his death would not lay a solid foundation for the country. The newly independent government's deliberate failure to convict Savarkar of Gandhi's murder gave Savarkar's followers a freer hand in revising his image. Since Savarkar's own death in 1966, a broader movement has risen from his ideology.

The RSS, which slavishly followed Savarkar and whose member Nathuram Godse shot Gandhi to death, has become the second largest political movement in the world after the Chinese Communist Party.[276] Using Savarkar's ideology of Hindutva, the RSS created a cluster of Hindu nationalist groups. The RSS "family" includes the Bharatiya Janata Party (BJP), which became the driving power of India's coalition government from 1998 to 2004.[277]

Once the BJP took power through a ruthless, anti-Muslim strategy,[278] it set out to rewrite history. BJP writers revised school textbooks to convey a Hindu nationalist slant in the history of India. Some things were better left unsaid. The new history books simply omitted Gandhi's assassination by RSS member Godse.[279]

The BJP also used its power in Delhi to revise the dark history of its ideological source, recreating Savarkar as a brave patriot. On May 4, 2002, BJP leader L. K. Advani, who had become the government's home minister, officially renamed Port Blair airport in the Andaman Islands as "Veer Savarkar Airport."[280] The government then unveiled a plaque in honor of Savarkar at the site of his cell in the prison at Port Blair.[281] In 2003, the government placed Savarkar's portrait in the Central Hall of Parliament House in New Delhi.[282] The BJP was trying to transform Savarkar in the public mind from the mastermind of Gandhi's murder into a mythical liberator of the country.

Nehru's rejection of Gandhi's legacy was completed by his support for the secret development of nuclear weapons for India. In a little-noted 1946 speech in Bombay, the soon-to-be prime minister began to envision a nuclear-armed India. He said:

> As long as the world is constituted as it is, every country will have to devise and use the latest scientific devices for its protection…. I hope Indian scientists will use the atomic force for constructive purposes. But if India is threatened she will inevitably try to defend herself by all means at her disposal.[283]

As prime minister, Nehru worked quietly to place the means of nuclear weapons at India's disposal, while stating publicly that he opposed them in all countries. His government established the Indian Atomic Energy Commission (AEC) on August 10, 1948,[284] laying the foundation, half a year after Gandhi's assassination, for India to become a nuclear weapons state.

The Atomic Energy Act that Nehru pushed through his Constituent Assembly "imposed even greater secrecy over research and development," as one analyst observed, "than did either the British or the American atomic energy legislation."[285] While claiming India's pursuit of nuclear power would be only for peaceful purposes, Nehru said, "Of course, if we are compelled as a nation to use it for other purposes, possibly no pious sentiments of any of us will stop the nation from using it that way."[286]

As Nehru knew, Gandhi had not expressed "pious sentiments" against nuclear weapons. He saw them realistically as threatening the extinction of the human race. Humanity was at a crossroad. India's pursuit of nuclear weapons would mean a walk down the road to destruction. Nonviolence was the alter-native. "Nonviolence," Gandhi said, "is the only thing the atom bomb cannot destroy."[287] But Gandhi was no longer there to point the way.

Nehru seemed to be upholding Gandhi's legacy. In the 1950s, he became internationally known as a proponent of nuclear dis-armament. In 1954 he became the first head of state to propose the cessation of nuclear testing.[288] Yet his attitude toward India's acquisition of nuclear weapons was more nuanced. Nehru said, in response to the possibility of India having to face a bordering, nuclear-armed state: "We have the technical know-how for man-ufacturing the atom bomb. We can do it in three or four years if we divert sufficient resources in that direction. But, we have given the world an assurance that we shall never do so."[289] The prime minister's pointed reference to his government's latent capacity to make a bomb, analyst George Perkovich has written, "can be interpreted as an early evocation of nuclear deterrence by India."[290]

Perkovich has documented how Nehru worked secretly with his longtime AEC chairman Homi Bhabha to research and develop India's capacity to make an atomic bomb.[291] When India actually exploded its first nuclear bomb on May 18, 1974, a decade after Nehru's death, at the order of his equally pro-nuclear daughter, Prime Minister Indira Gandhi,[292] his atomic legacy triumphed tragically over his teacher Gandhi's nonviolent hope for India as an instrument for world peace.[293]

Gandhi was assassinated half a year after India gained its independence through his leadership. The father of the country who sought a radically different future for India was gone. The nonviolent vision Gandhi opened up to the country was based on a power his old disciples, India's new rulers, could not accept, unless they were willing to reject the kind of nation-state handed over to them by the British. They accepted instead a kind of power that, in relation to Gandhi's assassination, was and is unspeakable. Gandhi's nonviolent vision of *swaraj,* which had brought them independence, was incompatible with the rise of their own national security state.

Their contradiction is our own. Gandhi's nonviolent revolution of the poor, loving and blessing the enemy all the way to a new future, is a truth we have not yet realized. Nor can we realize that truth so long as we accept its antithesis, a national security state protecting our affluence and dominance by nuclear weapons.

In the course of his experiments with truth, Gandhi discovered there was a third choice besides state terrorism and revolutionary terrorism. *Satyagraha,* truth-force, was based on a harmony of means and ends. Gandhi saw "there is just the same inviolable connection between the means and the end as there is between the seed and the tree. We reap exactly as we sow."[294]

Those who sowed terrorism would reap terrorism. Gandhi saw that Savarkar's means of fighting for independence was a terrible mistake. The Indian assassins of British officials would simply strengthen the systemic terrorism of the empire. And their violence, mirroring the violent means of the empire, would through Gandhi's assassination be carried over into the newly independent Indian government.

Gandhi and Savarkar posed two choices in opposing state power in the nuclear age: *satyagraha* or terrorism, experiments with a transforming power of truth or attempts to control others by whatever means available. The means would in either case become in the process their own ends.

Gandhi's death dramatized his commitment to a nonviolent vision that included yet transcended India. In his long journey that ended with his assassination, he sought God in the hearts of his enemies, including those who wanted to kill him. He chose to see his assassins as friends. They were, first of all, children of God. The triggermen, he pointed out in previous attempts on his life, were acting on the mistaken belief that they were doing the will of God. Even those who inspired them, or who gave them orders to kill, were not his main concern. Gandhi's real enemies, he knew, were not the triggermen, the plotters, or the ideologists of violence, but the unspeakable political and cultural forces they all obeyed as their gods.

Gandhi believed that all of us—no exceptions—could be liberated from our own violent prison by experiments in a universal power of truth and love.

His deepening willingness to confront his assassins with love was his last testament to us on the meaning of nonviolence. Gandhi's final experiment with truth was his death.

Gandhi, Godse, and the Cross

A paradox of Gandhi's assassination is that his beloved disciples, Jawaharlal Nehru and Vallabhbhai Patel, headed the Indian government under whose authority it occurred. Their government security forces were, by culpable inaction, complicit in the assassination. In the ten days following the January 20 attempt to kill Gandhi, that government's standard security measures were not carried out for the man regarded as the father of the nation.[1]

The police knew from their prisoner Madanlal Pahwa, from his employer and corroborating witness Professor Jain, and from surveillance of Savarkar's home everything necessary to stop the assassination. They knew the plot's target, who the gunmen were, and the probable mastermind as seen in the men's consultations with Savarkar. The police also knew the urgency of action. They had Madanlal's prediction: "They will come again."[2] Yet following the assassins' failure to kill Gandhi on the 20th, the remaining conspirators were left free to regroup and return. Godse, Apte, and Karkare used the second chance they were given by carrying out the murder of Gandhi on the 30th. Gandhi was killed in a vacuum of government security.

Nehru and Patel were devastated by Gandhi's assassination. The man who made them his lieutenants in a nonviolent revolution was in his final day on earth trying to keep his bickering

103

disciples together in a government he questioned. His martyrdom revived Nehru's and Patel's commitment to govern India
together, as they would until Patel's death not quite three years
later.

However, another consequence of Gandhi's death was to
relieve the prime minister and the home minister from the pressures of their teacher's conscience, as applied to their new pow-
ers of state. The state was not Gandhian. The government that
the British passed on was more consistent with imperial rule than
it was with a nonviolent independence movement. The Congress
Party leaders now headed the same structure of army, courts,
and police that had imprisoned them and over 100,000 other
civil resisters. Elements in that violent structure were especially
hostile to their leader, Gandhi.

Gandhi's assassins were investigated (even while they prepared the crime), arrested (after it), and tried by a judicial system that reflected in unacknowledged ways the political power of
Savarkar and the forces behind him. Before the murder, the police
would not arrest Savarkar. They feared the political reaction. In
the murder trial, the prosecution refrained from following the
evidence against Savarkar. The government backed away from
the responsibility of presenting its full case against Savarkar,
lest he be convicted. As Bombay Home Minister Morarji Desai
put it in his (judicially deleted) testimony, "Shall I give the full
facts?... It is for [Savarkar] to decide," as to what evidence Desai
would present against him.[3] Before the murder and later in the
trial, government authorities deferred to the power they could
see behind the plot. As a result, Gandhi was killed, and the truth
was covered up.

The assassins, who carried out a fierce ideological mandate in
their murder of Gandhi, had their sympathizers in the system. In
the furies of partition, powerful anti-Gandhi attitudes had grown
within India's security apparatus. Nehru and Patel headed the
government, but they did not control all its tentacles. That was
another price of accepting power in a growing national security
bureaucracy—edging toward complicity in unspeakable crimes,
as Nehru, Patel, and their nuclear-armed successors would do.

What may highlight Gandhi's nonviolence more than Nehru's and Patel's departures from it as India's rulers is the courtroom attack made upon it by assassin Nathuram Godse. For Godse, as for his mentor, Savarkar, it was not enough to kill Gandhi in the flesh. Their deeper purpose was to destroy the spirit of Gandhi. From their standpoint, Gandhi's nonviolence would mean the death of India.

Savarkar, maintaining what the CIA would call "plausible deniability,"[4] stayed in the shadows behind his shooters, Madan-lal Dhingra (in London) and Nathuram Godse (in Delhi). Godse's courtroom statement was a Savarkarian indictment of Gandhi's nonviolent vision. Godse and Savarkar wanted to remove any influence Gandhi might have from the grave.

In explaining why he killed Gandhi, Godse said:

> I firmly believed that the teachings of absolute "Ahimsa" as advocated by Gandhiji would ultimately result in the emasculation of the Hindu community and thus make the community incapable of resisting the aggression or inroads of other communities, especially the Muslims....
>
> In 1946 or thereabout, the Muslim atrocities perpetrated on the Hindus, under the government patronage of Suhrawardy in Noakhali, made our blood boil. Our shame and indignation knew no bounds when we saw that Gandhiji had come forward to shield that very Suhrawardy.[5]

Godse, covering for Savarkar, did not disclose that Suhrawardy and Nehru were actually assassination targets with Gandhi, in an order from Savarkar that all three should be "finished."[6] But Godse's courtroom statement repeatedly singled out the scandal of Gandhi's reaching out to the notorious Suhrawardy, acknowledged by the shooter as a reason for the murder.

Godse said:

> A little more than two weeks before Pandit Nehru was to take office [in the provisional government of India], there broke out in Calcutta an open massacre of the Hindus which continued for three days unchecked.... At the time

it was considered that the government which could permit such outrages on its citizens must be thrown out; there
were actual suggestions that Mr. Suhrawardy's government
should be dismissed.... Gandhiji, however, went to Calcutta and contracted a strange friendship with the author
of these massacres.[7]

Godse went on to claim in a historical overview that Gandhi,
by his returning to India from South Africa, rather than leading India to independence actually delayed its achievement:
"Gandhiji arrived in India in 1914-15. Nearly eight years earlier, the revolutionary movement had spread over a large part of
India.... After the arrival of Gandhiji and his fads of truth and
nonviolence, the movement began to suffer eclipse."[8]

Progress toward India's freedom would have come instead,
Godse believed, from terrorism: "From 1906 till 1918 one Brit-
isher after another and his Indian stooges were shot dead by the
revolutionary nationalists, and the British authorities were trem-
bling about their very existence."[9]

Godse then paid tribute to a series of Indian proponents of
violent revolution and assassination, mentioning in particular Savarkar's London disciple, Madanlal Dhingra, who assassinated Sir Curzon Wyllie. These were true examples of "the
living protest by Indian youth against the alien yoke. They had
unfurled and held aloft the flag of independence, some of them
long before Gandhiji's name was heard of."[10]

Yet, to Godse's dismay in retrospect, Gandhi had condemned
unequivocally this wave of revolutionary violence: "Gandhiji
publicly denounced it day after day on every platform and
through the press."

"And the more the Mahatma condemned the use of force in
the country's battle for freedom," Godse claimed, "the more
popular it became."[11]

Returning to communal violence, Godse charged Gandhi with discouraging a natural, necessary Hindu retaliation
against the Muslims: "Gandhiji needed to take into consider-
ation that the desire for reprisals springing up in the Hindu

mind was simply a natural reaction…The retaliatory actions taken by the Hindus in Bihar and elsewhere were the inevitable outcome of the revulsion felt by the Hindus at the shocking atrocities in other provinces. Such a feeling is at times as spiritual and natural as that of kindness."[12]

Godse characterized his killing of Gandhi as part of a wider protection of society: "It would be quite impossible to put an end to the governance of society by the wicked, had it not been for such feelings of discontent, retaliation, and revenge springing up against wicked dictators."[13]

Moreover, he argued, following Savarkar's gospel, Gandhi's murder was vindicated by Indian mythology, modern war, and human nature: "The events of ancient history as depicted in *The Ramayana* and *Mahabharata*, or the more modern wars of England and America against Germany and Japan, also indicate the same sort of action and reaction. It may be either good or bad. Such is human nature."[14]

Godse presented his themes celebrating his murder of Gandhi with the proud claim that history was on his side. To those who reject his action, Godse says, we may not want to admit it in this particular case but history vindicates his principles:

(1) Nonviolence is incapable of resisting aggression. As government policy, it would destroy a country.

(2) Befriending an enemy such as Suhrawardy, responsible for atrocities against our people, is wrong. The enemy should be killed.

(3) To win or preserve freedom, killing must be done, including assassinations and the other tactics of modern warfare.

(4) Violence in retaliation against the wicked is simply human nature. Retribution in fact makes it possible to govern society.

Even if we reject the way Godse applied his principles to carry out Gandhi's murder, he is suggesting we may share his beliefs. If the assassin's shoe fits, he says, wear it.

Is it possible we share more of Gandhi's beliefs than Godse's? While Gandhi was saying to the English people that their empire was wrong, he was also suggesting that at the heart of their Christianity were beliefs that could transform the world nonviolently.

On Gandhi's voyage back to India after the Second Round Table Conference in London, the Christians attending his morning prayers made a request. It was Christmas Day 1931. The Christians asked their Hindu friend, Gandhi, if he would please speak to them about Jesus.

Gandhi responded:

> I shall tell you how, to an outsider like me, the story of Christ, as told in the *New Testament*, has struck. My acquaintance with the *Bible* began nearly forty-five years ago, and that was through the *New Testament*....When I came to the *New Testament* and the Sermon on the Mount, I began to understand the Christian teaching, and the teaching of the Sermon on the Mount echoed something I had learned in childhood and something which seemed to be part of my being....
>
> This teaching was non-retaliation or non-resistance to evil. Of all the things I read, what remained with me forever was that Jesus came almost to give a new law—though he, of course, had said he had not come to give a new law, but tack something on to the old Mosaic law. Well, he changed it so that it became a new law—not an eye for an eye, and a tooth for a tooth, but to be ready to receive two blows when only one was given, and to go two miles when you were asked to go one....
>
> As my contact with real Christians, i.e., people living in fear of God increased, I saw that the Sermon on the Mount was the whole of Christianity for one who wanted to live a Christian life. It is that sermon which has endeared Jesus to me....
>
> Reading the whole story in the light [of the Sermon on the Mount], it seems to me that Christianity has yet to be lived, unless one says that where there is boundless love and no idea of retaliation whatsoever, it is Christianity that

lives. But then it surmounts all boundaries and book teaching. Then it is something indefinable, not capable of being preached to men, not capable of being transmitted from mouth to mouth, but from heart to heart. But Christianity is not commonly understood in that way.

Somehow, in God's providence, the *Bible* has been preserved from destruction by the Christians, so-called.... Two thousand years in the life of a living faith may be nothing. For though we sang, "All glory to God on high and on the earth be peace," there seems to be today neither glory to God nor peace on earth.

As long as it remains a hunger still unsatisfied, as long as Christ is not yet born, we have to look forward to him. When real peace is established, we will not need demonstrations, but it will be echoed in our life, not only in individual life, but in corporate life. Then we shall say Christ is born. That to me is the real meaning of the verse we have sung. Then we will not think of a particular day in the year as that of the birth of the Christ, but as an ever-recurring event which can be enacted in every life....

When, therefore, one wishes "a happy Christmas" without the meaning behind it, it becomes nothing more than an empty formula. And unless one wishes for peace for all life, one cannot wish for peace for oneself. It is a self-evident axiom, like the axioms of Euclid, that one cannot have peace unless there is in one an intense longing for peace all around. You may certainly experience peace in the midst of strife, but that happens only when to remove strife you destroy your whole life, you crucify yourself.

And so, as the miraculous birth is an eternal event, so is the cross an eternal event in this stormy life. Therefore, we dare not think of birth without death on the cross. Living Christ means a living cross, without it life is a living death.[15]

On the eve of the Second World War, in the late autumn of 1938, an international group of Christians met in Madras in southeast India to discuss how they might make decisions "in the light of the message of Christ."[16] A number of them traveled an extra distance so that they might "sit at the feet of a Hindu leader, Mr. Gandhi. Their object was to gain from him advice as to how they might learn to follow Christ better."[17]

In Gandhi's conversations with the Christians, he dealt first with Jesus' view of money. He said:

> I think you cannot serve God and mammon both.... I have always felt that when a religious organization has more money than it requires, it is in peril of losing its faith in God, and pinning its faith on money. You have simply to cease to depend on it.
>
> In South Africa, when I started the satyagraha march, there was not a copper in my pocket, and I went with a light heart. I had a caravan of 3,000 people to support. "No fear," said I. "If God wills it, He will carry it forward." Then money began to rain from India. I had to stop it, for when the money came, my miseries began.... *The fact is, the moment financial stability is assured, spiritual bankruptcy is also assured.* (Gandhi's emphasis)[18]

The Christians asked Gandhi what they should do with "gangster nations." They had in mind their threatening opponents in Germany, Italy, and Japan, though in the eyes of Indians and other subject peoples, the rulers of the British Empire might also have qualified.

Gandhi said: "Ultimately force, however justifiably used, will lead us into the same morass as the force of Hitler and Mussolini. There will be just a difference of degree. Those who believe in nonviolence must use it at the critical moment. We must not despair of touching the heart even of gangsters, even though for the moment we may seem to be striking our heads against a blind wall."[19]

Gandhi's pre-war comment to the Christians was the same in substance as his post-war response to Vincent Sheean's dismay at the war's consequences seen in a nuclear arms race: "Your ends [in the war] may have been good but your means were bad. That is not the way of truth."

"Nonviolence," Gandhi told Sheean after the war, just as he told the Christians before it, "is absolutely necessary for a good result."[20]

Gandhi was speaking from experience. What he discovered from his experiments with truth to the point of death was a universal truth. He was telling the Christians they might be able to recognize it. The moral structure of reality corresponded not to the principles of the rulers of Germany, Italy, Japan, nor even those of the British Empire. Cosmic reality, he saw, was rooted in the truth of what he called "the cross."

As a reporter of Gandhi's dialogue with the Christians observed, Gandhi was suggesting "the rediscovery of the cross, not as a dogma, but as a living and eternal principle for the ending of wrong, warfare, violence."[21]

Gandhi saw a total equation between nonviolence and the power behind the universe. He told the statesmen:

In my opinion, nonviolence is not passivity in any shape or form. Nonviolence, as I understand it, is the most active force in the world.... Nonviolence is the supreme law. During my half-century of experience, I have not yet come across a situation when I had to say that I was helpless, that I had no remedy in terms of nonviolence.[22]

Gandhi also saw that the residual power within people far exceeded what Christian politicians assumed as a basis for their decisions. He quoted the lines from Percy Bysshe Shelley's poem, *Mask of Anarchy*, which ended as follows:

Rise like lions after slumber
In unvanquishable number –
Shake your chains to earth, like dew
Which in sleep has fallen on you—
Ye are many, they are few.[23]

Before Gandhi's visitors departed, he gave them a prime example of the nonviolence he meant. It came from that part of the Muslim world that would preoccupy U.S. military planners of drone and special-forces assassination attacks in the twenty-first century. Gandhi described what he had witnessed among the Muslim nonviolent soldiers led by Abdul Ghaffar Khan in the North-West Frontier Province of India (that would become a part of Pakistan after India's partition):

I was not prepared for what I saw. They are in dead earnest about the thing, and there is a deep-rooted sincerity in their hearts. They themselves see light and hope in nonviolence…. Before it was all darkness. There was not a family but had its blood feuds. They lived like tigers in a den. Though the Pathans used to be always armed with knives, daggers, and rifles, they used to be terrified of their superior officers, lest they should lose their jobs. All that has changed now with thousands. Blood feuds are becoming a thing of the past among those Pathans who have come under the influence of Khansaheb's nonviolence movement.[24]

Gandhi's final statement to the Christians was about prayer:

We have joint worship morning and evening at 4:20 am and 7 pm. This has gone on for years. We have a recitation of verses from the *Gita* and other accepted religious books, also hymns of saints, with or without music. Individual worship cannot be described in words. It goes on continuously and even unconsciously. There is not a moment when I do not feel the presence of a Witness, whose eye misses nothing, and with whom I strive to keep in tune. I do not pray as Christian friends do, not because I think there is anything wrong in it; but because words won't come to me. I suppose it is a matter of habit…. God knows and anticipates our wants. The Deity does not need my supplication; but I, a very imperfect human being, do need His protection as a child that of its father…. I have never found Him lacking in response. I have found Him nearest at hand when the horizon seemed darkest—in my ordeals in jails, when it was not all smooth sailing for me.

I cannot recall a moment in my life when I had a sense of desertion by God.[25]

Gandhi's fundamental conviction about nonviolence was restated by his martyred successor, Martin Luther King, Jr., when he said, "Let us realize the arc of the moral universe is long but it bends toward justice."[26]

Martin Luther King also put Gandhi's basic question before us in the form of a contingent prophecy: "The choice today is no longer between violence and nonviolence. It is either nonviolence or nonexistence."[27]

That choice is ours.

Acknowledgments

I began the introduction by saying I never planned to write a book about Gandhi. Yet looking back from the end, I have to acknowledge the spiritual presence of Gandhi in just about everything I have written for half a century. The subject has been Jesus' nonviolence, but Gandhi has been my way into Jesus.

I discovered Gandhi during my studies at Santa Clara University in the 1950s. As my writing's focus after my graduation became Jesus' nonviolent cross, what Gandhi termed "experiments with truth" became my way to understand Jesus. Research, writing, and above all, nonviolent Gandhian campaigns with my wife, Shelley, and a series of inspiring communities have been the laboratories. As Gandhi said, "Truth is God." And as Jesus proclaimed, "The reign of God is at hand." The reign of God's will is no farther away than our hands. It is the focus of Jesus' prayer: "Thy will be done on earth as it is in heaven." Praying with our hands and feet, experimenting with the truths of our nonviolent faith step by step, in all things, big and small, is the Gandhian way. So thank you, Mohandas, for sharing your transforming way of acting on the truths we hold most deeply.

Seeking the truth of Gandhi's assassination has meant seeing his life through the eyes of those who knew him. I am grateful for the eyes of Narayan Desai, son of Gandhi's secretary, Mahadev Desai. Shelley and I met Narayan, who incarnates the spirit of Gandhi, when he visited us at Ground Zero Center for Nonviolent Action beside the Trident submarine base near Seattle in the 1980s. Narayan's four-volume biography of Gandhi, *My Life Is My Message*, and his biography of his father, Mahadev, *The Fire and the Rose*, have provided illuminating ways of seeing

Gandhi's and his disciples' encounters with death. I learned especially from the story of Mahadev Desai's sacrifice of his own life as a disciple, thereby turning Gandhi away from the ultimate temptation of giving his life prematurely.

I thank John Dear for initiating this pilgrimage by telling me of Arun Gandhi's knowledge of his grandfather's assassination. When I asked Arun whose writing he would recommend on Gandhi's death, he led me to his son, Tushar Gandhi. I studied Tushar's mammoth work, *Let's Kill Gandhi!*, paragraph by paragraph, as a way into the labyrinth. I also thank Arun and Tushar for their interviews, which further defined the journey ahead.

I am deeply grateful to the friends who read patiently and critiqued my work in progress: Bob and Janet Aldridge, Frank Bognar, Dennis Dalton, Narayan Desai, Arun Gandhi, Emmett Jarrett (with great generosity shortly before his death), Richard Johnson, Roger Ludwig, William Hart McNichols, Chris Moore-Backman, Don Mosley, Michael Nagler, Randall Mullins, Sharon Pavelda, Laurie Raymond, Bert Sacks, Michael Sonnleitner, Michael True, Louie Vitale, Patrick Walsh, and Jerry Zawada.

Frank Bognar and his family have sustained this work all the way by their loving support. Numerous rare books, otherwise inaccessible to me, found their way to our mailbox through the kindness of Frank, Mary Ann, Bobby, Holly, and Nick. Frank has been my consultant and resource person on countless research queries.

Rose Marie Berger and Julie Polter gave me warm hospitality in Washington, DC, and my sister- and brother-in-law Joann Hall and Larry McCormick in Alexandria, Virginia, while I studied the Gandhi murder trial evidence for a week at the U.S. Library of Congress. Dr. Meredith Shedd-Driskel, curator for the Law Library of Congress, facilitated my work with the eight volumes of the *Printed Record of the Mahatma Gandhi Murder Case*, formerly owned by Gandhi's assassin, Nathuram Godse, during the appeal of his death sentence. Catholic Worker Kathy Boylan put me in touch with photographer Tony DiChristoforo, who gave me his time and expertise in snapping clear pictures of hundreds of pages of the murder trial evidence. Ryan

Hamilton-Schumacher patiently prepared the foundations for the photographic work on this rare book before my departure from Birmingham, Alabama. On my return home, John Fievet kindly completed the digital work and printing of the pictures. For the entire DC trip, I experienced the grace of a support team made in heaven.

Rick Ambrose, John Fievet, and Jerry Levin have helped me through an electronic maze in the years since I put away my Royal portable typewriter. Rick's Internet research for sources beyond my reach was critical to my work on both JFK and Gandhi. In his final months on earth, Rick also critiqued this book insightfully.

On June 24, 2011, two days before Rick's death, we were talking about Gandhi.

"I'm only writing about Gandhi," I said. "You're about to meet him."

"Yes," said Rick, "and I hope it's soon."

I have dedicated the book to Rick, with a prayer for his even deeper help from the communion of saints.

Robert Ellsberg is my remarkably patient editor and publisher. When Robert saw the Gandhi chapters going beyond my intended introduction of Martin Luther King's and Malcolm X's stories, he asked quietly if that might not mean a book on Gandhi himself. I said no, but Robert was right. He often knows more than I do about where the words are going, and how to make a better book out of them. Thank you once again, Robert, for your guidance.

Shelley continues to be the best writer I know. That has made her my conscience in the many sentences that threatened to get out of hand. More important, during our forty-one years together, has been the presence of God's hope and joy in her eyes, in darkness and in light, through our experiments with the truths of our faith.

Notes

Introduction

1. After John Dear shared with me his information from Arun Gandhi about Gandhi's murder, I phoned Arun in November 2008 to learn more. Arun told me he had visited Gopal Godse several times in 1965-66, after Gopal served his "life sentence" (fourteen years in India) for being a conspirator in Gandhi's assassination. Gopal was the younger brother of Nathuram Godse, Gandhi's shooter, who was hanged with co-conspirator Narayan Apte on November 15, 1949. Arun said he expressed his forgiveness of Gopal in their meetings but that Gopal gave no sign of remorse for his role in the assassination. Gopal spoke openly to Arun about mastermind Vinayak Damodar Savarkar's having led and blessed the team of assassins. However, Savarkar was the only defendant who was found not guilty by Judge Atma Charan in the Gandhi murder trial, for reasons that will be explored here.

Arun recommended his son, Tushar A. Gandhi, as a resource person for more information. Tushar had written and compiled a 1,000-page sourcebook on his great-grandfather's assassination: *"Let's Kill Gandhi!": A Chronicle of His Last Days, the Conspiracy, Murder, Investigation and Trial* (New Delhi: Rupa, 2007). I read closely Tushar's comprehensive work, interviewed him on it, and studied the Gandhi murder trial evidence that is available at the U.S. Library of Congress: *Printed Record of Mahatma Gandhi Murder Case,* Vols. I-VIII (U.S. Library of Congress Law Library). This heavily annotated rare book once belonged to Nathuram Godse, whose signature is at the front of Vol. II.

An indispensable resource on the case is the Indian government's commission led by Judge J. L. Kapur, which in 1968-69 re-investigated the 1948 murder. Its report provides critical information on the murder conspiracy and police complicity not presented at the trial: J. L. Kapur, *Report of Commission of Inquiry into Conspiracy to Murder Mahatma Gandhi,* Vols. I-VIII (New Delhi: Ministry of Home Affairs, 1970).

These and the other sources I have cited draw a picture of Gandhi's assassination as a serious threat to Indian democracy, then and now, from forces that have profited from his murder.

2. Thomas Merton, *Raids on the Unspeakable* (New York: New Directions, 1966), p. 5.

3. Ibid., p. 4.

4. Stewart Galanor, *Cover-up* (New York: Kestrel Books, 1998), pp. 57-77, 171-76.

5. Merton, *Raids*, p. 5.

6. Ibid.

7. The declassified audiotapes of the White House meetings during the Cuban Missile Crisis reveal the intense pressures on President Kennedy to bomb the Soviet missile sites and invade Cuba. During Kennedy's October 19, 1962, meeting with his Joint Chiefs of Staff, Air Force General Curtis LeMay contemptuously dismissed the president's alternative of a blockade and political action as "almost as bad as the appeasement at Munich," a reference to the notorious 1938 conference at which Britain compelled Czechoslovakia to cede territory to Hitler. As LeMay kept taunting him, the president rejected his military commanders' arguments for a quick, massive attack. He thanked them and left the room. In his absence, the unseen tape machine continued to record the Chiefs' rebellious remarks about their commander-in-chief and their own need to escalate the crisis. See Sheldon M. Stern, *Averting "The Final Failure": John F. Kennedy and the Secret Cuban Missile Crisis Meetings* (Stanford, CA: Stanford University Press, 2003), pp. 123, 129.

General LeMay's Air Force did try to escalate the conflict to nuclear war by carrying out threatening actions unauthorized by President Kennedy. In the course of the crisis, the Air Force ordered nuclear-armed bombers beyond their usual turnaround points toward the Soviet Union and test-fired an intercontinental ballistic missile. The provocations were designed to push the Soviets to a reaction, thereby counter-provoking an immediate all-out nuclear attack by superior U.S. forces, all without Kennedy's authorization. The president's resolution of the crisis with Khrushchev came none too soon. It infuriated the Joint Chiefs, who wanted war. Richard Rhodes, "The General and World War III," *New Yorker*, June 19, 1995, 58-59; Scott D. Sagan, *The Limits of Safety* (Princeton, NJ: Princeton University Press, 1993), p. 79.

Defense Secretary Robert McNamara recalled the Chiefs' outrage at Kennedy, superseding his gracious attitude toward them: "After Khrushchev had agreed to remove the missiles, President Kennedy invited the Chiefs to the White House so that he could thank them for their support during the crisis, and there was one hell of a scene. LeMay came out saying, 'We lost! We ought to just go in there today and knock 'em off!'" Rhodes, "General and World War III," p. 58.

8. President Kennedy used the phrase "the final failure" to turn a discussion away from war in a critical October 18, 1962, meeting of the Executive Committee of the National Security Council. When his advisors pushed the president to take steps in the crisis that seemed likely to result in nuclear war, JFK replied, "Now the question *really* is what action we take which *lessens* the chances of a nuclear exchange, which obviously is the final failure" (emphasis in original). *Averting "The Final Failure,"* pp. 105-6.

9. Kennedy's and Khrushchev's unlikely alliance, and their work for peace with Pope John XXIII, has been described by Norman Cousins in his book *The Improbable Triumvirate: John F. Kennedy, Pope John, Nikita Khrushchev* (New York: W. W. Norton, 1972). Cousins, the editor of the *Saturday Review* and a founder of SANE (National Committee for a Sane Nuclear Policy), served as a back-channel intermediary between the three leaders.

10. Thomas Merton's *Gandhi on Non-Violence: Selected Texts from Mohandas K. Gandhi's Non-Violence in Peace and War* (New York: New Directions, 1965), and *Raids on the Unspeakable* were published back to back in 1965 and 1966. Merton wrote his introductory essay to the Gandhi book, "Gandhi and the One-Eyed Giant," in April 1964. It laid a Gandhian foundation for his confrontation with the Unspeakable in *Raids*, whose essays he completed in late 1965. "With the approach of Christmas [1965] and the end of the year, Father Louis worked quietly on preparing *Raids on the Unspeakable* for publication and giving his attention to solitude." John Howard Griffin, *Follow the Ecstasy: The Hermitage Years of Thomas Merton* (Maryknoll, NY: Orbis Books, 1993), p. 41.

11. Thomas Merton, "Introduction: Gandhi and the One-Eyed Giant," in *Gandhi on Non-Violence,* p. 4.

12. Thomas Merton, "A Tribute to Gandhi," in *Seeds of Destruction* (New York: Farrar, Straus, & Giroux, 1964), p. 231.

13. Ibid., p. 233.

14. Merton introducing Gandhi's statements in the section on "The Spiritual Dimensions of Non-Violence," in *Gandhi on Non-Violence*, p. 43.

15. "Gandhi and the One-Eyed Giant," *Gandhi on Non-Violence*, p. 5.

16. Martha C. Nussbaum, *The Clash Within: Democracy, Religious Violence, and India's Future* (Cambridge, MA: Harvard University Press, 2007), pp. 165-70.

17. See concluding chapter here, "Gandhi, Godse, and the Cross," endnote 4.

Seeds of Life and Death

1. Cited by John Dear, *Mohandas Gandhi: Essential Writings* (Maryknoll, NY: Orbis Books, 2002), p. 143.

2. I am grateful to Gandhian scholar Michael Sonnleitner for his thoughtful critique of my original draft of the previous introductory paragraph. I have rewritten it, and one to come in the second chapter, in the light of his insights.

3. *Gandhi on Non-Violence: Selected Texts from Mohandas K. Gandhi's Non-Violence in Peace and War,* edited by Thomas Merton (New York: New Directions, 1965), p. 68.

4. M. K. Gandhi, *An Autobiography or the Story of My Experiments with Truth, Book One* (Ahmedabad: Navajivan Press, 1927), p. 166.

5. Maureen Swan, *Gandhi: The South African Experience* (Johannesburg: Ravan Press, 1985), p. 60.

6. Pyarelal, *Mahatma Gandhi: II, The Discovery of Satyagraha— On the Threshold* (Bombay: Sevak Prakashan, 1980), p. 74.

7. Ibid.

8. Ibid., p. 46.

9. *Autobiography*, pp. 282-83.

10. Pyarelal, *Mahatma Gandhi: II, The Discovery of Satyagraha*, pp. 48-53.

11. *Autobiography*, p. 284.

12. M. K. Gandhi, *Satyagraha in South Africa* (Ahmedabad: Navajivan, 1928), pp. 53-54.

13. Ibid., p. 54.

14. Louis Fischer, *The Life of Mahatma Gandhi* (New York: Collier

Books, 1950), p. 60; Pyarelal, *Mahatma Gandhi:* II, *The Discovery of Satyagraha,* pp. 56-57.

15. Narayan Desai, *My Life Is My Message:* I, *Sadhana (1869-1915)* (New Delhi: Orient Blackswan, 2009), p. 172.

16. Ibid., p. 201.

17. M. K. Gandhi, *Satyagraha in South Africa*, pp. 58-59.

18. *Autobiography*, p. 289.

19. Gandhi, *Satyagraha in South Africa*, p. 57.

20. Pyarelal, *Mahatma Gandhi:* II, *The Discovery of Satyagraha,* pp. 282-83.

21. Ibid., p. 284.

22. Gandhi, *Satyagraha in South Africa*, p. 96.

23. Ibid., pp. 97-100.

24. Ibid., p. 102. Gandhi was careful to distinguish *satyagraha* from passive resistance. He was first moved to do so when a European friend introduced him for a presentation in a way that shocked him. The man said that because the Transvaal Indians could not vote, were only a few, and had no weapons, "therefore they have taken to passive resistance which is a weapon of the weak."

In a chapter on "Satyagraha v. Passive Resistance" in *Satyagraha in South Africa*, Gandhi countered the idea that *satyagraha* was a weapon of the weak: "Although the Indians had no franchise and were weak [in number], these considerations had nothing to do with the organization of Satyagraha.... My point is that I can definitely assert that in planning the Indian movement there never was the slightest thought given to the possibility or otherwise of offering armed resistance. Satyagraha is soul force pure and simple."

Gandhi thought that, because of the power of suggestion, it was especially important for the Indians to identify their movement correctly: "If we continue to believe ourselves and let others believe, that we are weak and helpless and therefore offer passive resistance, our resistance would never make us strong, and at the earliest opportunity we would give up passive resistance as a weapon of the weak. On the other hand if we are Satyagrahis and offer Satyagraha believing ourselves to be strong, two clear consequences result from it. Fostering the idea of strength, we grow stronger and stronger every day.... Again, while there is no scope for love in passive resistance, on the other hand not only has hatred no place in Satyagraha but is a positive breach of its ruling principle. While in passive resistance there is a scope for the use of arms when a suitable occasion arrives, in Satyagraha physical force is forbidden even in the most favorable circumstances.... In passive resistance there is always present an idea of harassing the other party ... while in Satyagraha there is not the remotest idea of injuring the opponent. Satyagraha postulates the conquest of the adversary by suffering in one's own person." Gandhi, *Satyagraha in South Africa*, pp. 103-6.

25. Rajmohan Gandhi, *Gandhi: The Man, His People, and the Empire* (Berkeley: University of California Press, 2008), pp. 119-21.

26. Gandhi, *Satyagraha in South Africa*, p. 144.

27. Ibid., p. 146.

28. Ibid., p. 147.

29. Ibid., p. 148.

30. Ibid.

31. Ibid., p. 149. R. Gandhi, *Gandhi: The Man, His People, and the Empire*, p. 123.

32. Gandhi, *Satyagraha in South Africa*, p. 150.

33. Ibid.

34. Ibid., p. 154.

35. *The Collected Works of Mahatma Gandhi* (New Delhi: Publications Division Government of India, 1999), 98 volumes. Vol. 8, p. 154. *Indian Opinion*, February 22, 1908.

36. Joseph Lelyveld's interview with Thambi Naidoo's grandson, Prema Naidoo, Johannesburg, November 2007; Joseph Lelyveld, *Great Soul: Mahatma Gandhi and His Struggle with India* (New York: Alfred A. Knopf, 2011), p. 85.

37. *Autobiography*, pp. 28, 45-46.

38. M. K. Gandhi, *Ramanama* (Ahmedabad: Navajivan, 1949), pp. 14-15.

39. Pyarelal, *Mahatma Gandhi: The Last Phase*, II (Ahmedabad: Navajivan, 1956), p. 773.

40. Gandhi, *Satyagraha in South Africa*, p. 154. Although Gandhi opposed the prosecution of Mir Alam and the Pathan companions who assaulted him, he responded privately in a different way to a man behind the assaults on two other leaders of the *satyagraha* movement. Gandhi became alarmed at how he thought the Pathan community was being manipulated by one behind-the-scenes member into carrying out a series of attacks. He then wrote to Smuts in May 1908 asking the government's help in a way that seemed to contradict his public stand against prosecution: "Many more may be assaulted in the near future.... The most violent member of the Pathan community, who has remained behind the scenes but who has been an active agent in

having the assaults committed, has been arrested today on a charge of inspiring to do harm. If it is at all possible, I certainly think that this man should be deported. In my opinion he is more or less a maniac and many dissatisfied Indians simply hang around him ... you will add to the peace of mind of well-behaved Indians ... by dealing with the fanatic I have mentioned either by way of deportation or by treating him as a prohibited immigrant under the Immigrants' Restriction Act. I believe he possesses no documents." Gandhi to Smuts, May 21, 1908. Cited by Maureen Swan, *Gandhi: South African Experience*, p. 163. Gandhi's reporting of the man to Smuts did not have the desired effect. The government did not deport him, but did arrest two of the "ring-leaders." Ibid., p. 186.

Gandhi's renunciation of prosecution in the case of Mir Alam did not mean he thought nonviolence and forgiveness required that one never bring a violent person to law. While embracing an ethic of forgiveness, Gandhi recognized that the common good could justify a government's arresting and jailing someone convicted of a violent crime. A humane confinement in jail, along with genuine efforts at rehabilitation, could, for example, be looked at as the adult equivalent of a child's "time out." Yet Gandhi would have been horrified at the prison industrial system in the United States that keeps over three million people in prison and carries out state executions. I am grateful to my friend Bert Sacks for raising the question of Gandhi's underlying attitude toward prosecution.

41. R. Gandhi, *Gandhi: The Man, His People, and the Empire*, p. 124.

42. Gandhi, *Satyagraha in South Africa*, pp. 174-75.

43. Robert Payne, *The Life and Death of Mahatma Gandhi* (New York: E. P. Dutton, 1969), p. 190.

44. Ibid., p. 189. R. Gandhi, *Gandhi: The Man, His People, and the Empire*, p. 126.

45. R. Gandhi, *Gandhi: The Man, His People, and the Empire*, p. 126.

46. Millie Graham Polak, *Mr. Gandhi: The Man* (London: George Allen & Unwin, 1931), pp. 102-3.

47. R. Gandhi, *Gandhi: The Man, His People, and the Empire*, p. 129.

48. Swan, *Gandhi: South African Experience*, p. 236.

49. Ibid.

50. R. Gandhi, *Gandhi: The Man, His People, and the Empire*, p. 162.

51. Desai, *My Life Is My Message,* I, p. 313.

52. Ibid., p. 314.

53. Swan, *Gandhi: South African Experience,* p. 247.

54. Ibid., p. 249.

55. Ibid., p. 250.

56. Ibid.

57. Gandhi, *Satyagraha in South Africa,* p. 273.

58. R. Gandhi, *Gandhi: The Man, His People, and the Empire,* p. 167.

59. Fischer, *The Life of Mahatma Gandhi,* p. 121.

60. Geoffrey Ashe, *Gandhi* (New York: Scarborough Books, 1980), p. 124.

61. Ibid.

62. Gandhi, *Satyagraha in South Africa,* p. 295.

63. Michael W. Sonnleitner, "The Birth of Gandhian *Satyagraha*: Nonviolent Resistance and Soul Force," in *Gandhi's Experiments with Truth: Essential Writings by and about Mahatma Gandhi,* ed. Richard L. Johnson (Lanham, MD: Rowman & Littlefield, 2006), p. 171.

64. Desai, *My Life Is My Message,* I, p. 578.

65. Ibid.

66. Ibid.

67. In an essay on Gandhi, Nelson Mandela wrote, "Gandhi threatened the South African Government during the first and second decades of our century as no other man did. He established the first anti-colonial political organization in the country, if not in the world, founding the Natal Indian Congress in 1894. The African People's Organization (APO) was established in 1902, the ANC in 1912, so that both were witnesses to and highly influenced by Gandhi's militant *satyagraha* which began in 1907 and reached its climax in 1913 with the epic march of 5000 workers indentured on the coal mines of Natal.... That [march] was the beginning of the marches to freedom and mass stay-away-from-work which became so characteristic of our freedom struggle in the apartheid era. Our Defiance Campaign of 1952, too, followed very much on the lines that Gandhi had set." Nelson Mandela, "Gandhi the Prisoner: A Comparison," in *Mahatma Gandhi: 125 Years,* ed. B. R. Nanda (New Delhi: Indian Council for Cultural Relations, 1995), p. 8.

68. Gandhi, *Satyagraha in South Africa,* p. 181.

69. Robert A. Huttenback, *Gandhi in South Africa: British Imperialism and the Indian Question, 1860-1914* (Ithaca, NY: Cornell Univer-

sity Press, 1971), p. 330; W. K. Hancock, *Smuts: The Sanguine Years, 1870-1919* (Cambridge: Cambridge University Press, 1962), p. 345.

70. J. C. Smuts, "Gandhi's Political Method," in *Mahatma Gandhi: Essays and Reflections on His Life and Work*, ed. S. Radhakrishnan (Bombay: Jaico, 1956), p. 217.

71. Charles McMoran Wilson Moran, *Churchill: The Struggle for Survival; Taken from the Diaries of Lord Moran, 1940-1965* (Boston: Houghton Mifflin, 1966), p. 57.

72. Ibid.

Gandhi and His Assassins

1. Dhingra's father, Sahib Ditta Mal, and his family in India had become alarmed by reports that Madanlal was staying at India House in London, known as a center of militant student activism. Madanlal's eldest brother, while on a visit to England, had then written to their highly placed family friend, Sir William Curzon Wyllie, asking if he would reach out to Madanlal with some guidance. On April 13, 1909, Wyllie wrote his own letter to Madanlal, saying he had received a letter from his brother "asking me to be of any assistance I can to you." Madanlal, who had become a devoted follower of the virulently anti-British Savarkar, ignored the letter from Wyllie, now identified as an enemy. He suspected his family's friend was having him shadowed. Two and a half months later, following Savarkar's orders, Madanlal stalked Wyllie and shot him to death. V. N. Datta, *Madan Lal Dhingra and the Revolutionary Movement* (New Delhi: Vikas, 1978), p. 46. Harindra Srivastava, *Five Stormy Years: Savarkar in London; June 1906—June 1911* (New Delhi: Allied Publishers, 1983), p. 148.

2. Datta, *Madan Lal Dhingra*, pp. 34-35; Srivastava, *Five Stormy Years*, p. 147.

3. Ibid., p. 151. We know of Savarkar's direct order to Dhingra to kill Wyllie because "to his biographer Dhananjay Keer, who wrote an account of Savarkar and his times, [Savarkar] claimed full credit for the murder." Robert Payne, *The Life and Death of Mahatma Gandhi* (New York: E. P. Dutton, 1969), p. 617; see Dhananjay Keer, *Veer Savarkar* (Bombay: Popular Prakashan, 1966), p. 53.

4. Srivastava, *Five Stormy Years*, 147.

5. Ibid., p. 168.

6. James D. Hunt, *Gandhi in London* (New Delhi: Promilla,

1978), p. 134; Rajmohan Gandhi, *Gandhi: The Man, His People, and the Empire* (Berkeley: University of California Press, 2007), p. 139; Dhananjay Keer, *Mahatma Gandhi: Political Saint and Unarmed Prophet* (Bombay: Popular Prakashan, 1973), p. 153.

7. On July 4, 1909, three days after Wyllie's assassination, about twelve members of Savarkar's revolutionary group met at India House. An undercover Scotland Yard agent infiltrated the meeting and reported on it.

Everyone at the meeting knew that the leader, Savarkar, had deliberately absented himself from the scene of Dhingra's murder of Wyllie, thereby making himself less culpable. One of Savarkar's lieutenants, Koregaonkar, had accompanied Dhingra to the reception, spurring him on to shoot Wyllie at the appropriate moment.

At the July 4th meeting, those present took turns paying tribute to Savarkar as the actual author of the assassination. One said, "Dhingra was the product of Savarkar's sound teaching." Savarkar himself said with satisfaction, "Dhingra stood cool and calm, firing at the prostrate figure of his country's enemy, Wyllie."

Although the Scotland Yard report concluded that Dhingra's murder of Wyllie was apparently "engineered by Savarkar" with the aid of three lieutenants, the British government charged only Dhingra with the crime. Lord Morley, the Secretary of State for India, preferred to remove the others more quietly, by extradition, "from the highly sensitive and politically conscious atmosphere of London" to be dealt with in a more punitive way elsewhere. That would be the case with Savarkar, extradited from Britain for a murder committed by co-conspirators in India, resulting in his being tried and punished there. Government of India, Home Department, *Proceedings*, Political B, August 1909, Nos. 120-29. *Madan Lal Dhingra*, pp. 56-57, 79.

8. Srivastava, *Five Stormy Years*, p. 199.

9. *The Collected Works of Mahatma Gandhi* [hereafter cited as CWMG], IX (Ahmedabad: Navajivan Trust, 1968), p. 302. Gandhi's reference to *bhang* indicates his possible knowledge of the conspirators' preparation of Dhingra for his deed, at a restaurant just before he went to the Imperial Institute. Scotland Yard's Intelligence Report stated that Dhingra was "alleged to have been plied with *bhang* [by some of his associates], before setting out to commit the outrage." Government of India, Home Department, *Proceedings*, Political A, September 1909, Nos. 66-68. Datta, *Madan Lal Dhingra*, p. 54.

10. CWMG, IX, p. 303.

11. Ibid., p. 302; Srivastava, *Five Stormy Years*, pp. 175-76.

12. *Five Stormy Years*, p. 25. Hunt, *Gandhi in London*, p. 233.

13. "Revolt, bloodshed and revenge have often been instruments created by nature to root out injustice and introduce an era of justice ... indeed if there was no propensity in human nature towards a terrible revenge for an horrible injustice suffered, the brute in man would have been still the dominating factor in human dealings." Vinayak Damodar Savarkar, *The First Indian War of Independence, 1857*, pp. 217-19; cited by A. G. Noorani, *Savarkar and Hindutva: The Godse Connection* (New Delhi: Left Word Books, 2002), p. 44.

14. *CWMG*, IX, p. 302.

15. Srivastava, *Five Stormy Years*, p. 180.

16. Gandhi described the dinner in his October 29, 1909, letter to a friend, journalist Henry Polak. *CWMG*, IX, p. 504.

17. Srivastava, *Five Stormy Years*, p. 180.

18. Gandhi in his October 29, 1909, letter to Polak. *CWMG*, IX, p. 504.

19. Srivastava, *Five Stormy Years*, p. 180.

20. *CWMG*, IX, p. 498.

21. Ibid., p. 499. Emphasis added.

22. Ibid.

23. Gandhi in a letter to Lord Ampthill, October 30, 1909. *CWMG*, IX, p. 509.

24. Rajmohan Gandhi has characterized Gandhi's "reader" as "arguing along lines that Savarkar and London's militant students (and also [Gandhi's old friend, Pranjivan] Mehta) had employed." R. Gandhi, *Gandhi: The Man, His People, and the Empire*, p. 143. In 1940 Gandhi said he wrote *Hind Swaraj* "for my dear friend Dr. Pranjivan Mehta. All the argument in the book is reproduced almost as it took place with him"; cited by S. R. Mehrotra, "Introduction" to *Indian Home Rule (Hind Swaraj)* (New Delhi: Promilla Publishers, Centenary Edition, 2010), p. 9. Gandhi stayed with Pranjivan Mehta at a London hotel for a month in 1909, during his visit from South Africa when he met the same arguments for violence from Savarkar and the India House students. Whereas Mehta became a devoted supporter of Gandhi's nonviolence, Savarkar re-formulated his arguments for violence into Hindutva, making Gandhi their ultimate verbal and physical target.

25. *The Selected Works of Mahatma Gandhi: IV, The Basic Works, Hind Swaraj*, ed. Shriman Narayan (Ahmedabad: Navajivan, 1968), pp. 155-56, 159-63.

26. Srivastava, *Five Stormy Years*, p. 204.

27. Petition from V. D. Savarkar (Convict No. 32778) to the Home Member of the Government of India, dated November 14, 1913; cited by R. C. Majumdar, *Penal Settlement in Andamans* (New Delhi: Gazetters Unit, Department of Culture, Ministry of Education and Social Welfare, Government of India, 1975), p. 213. Also A. G. Noorani, "A National Hero?" *Frontline* 21, no. 22 (2004): 10. When the mass of political prisoners in the Cellular Jail carried out a general strike in civil disobedience to their brutal treatment, Vinayak Savarkar and his brother Barbarao did not join them. A fellow prisoner who took part in the strike, Trailokya Nath Chakravarty, observed in his description of the struggle, "[The Savarkar brothers], who came before us and suffered the same miseries, had wrung some concessions and privileges after a hard fight [in a previous strike] and were now favorites of the Superintendent; so they were not prepared to renounce them and join us in our struggle." Trailokya Nath Chakravarty, *Jele Tris Bachar* ("*Thirty Years in Jail*"), cited by Majumdar, *Penal Settlement,* p. 238. Vinayak Savarkar, in his own account, claimed that his leadership position in the national movement required that he not join the strike: "To risk one's life for such a petty object was to kill the national movement itself.... Hence it was for the young and the energetic among us to shoulder the burden, and these hundred and odd persons must by turns keep up the agitation and all the activities connected with it." Savarkar added that "the most important reason for my abstaining from [the strike] was that I would have forfeited my right of sending a letter [once a year] to India," whose influence he thought would be more beneficial to the other prisoners than his joining them in the strike. Vinayak Damodar Savarkar, *The Story of My Transportation for Life: A Biography of Black Days of Andamans*; English translation of Savarkar's 1947 Marathi-language book, *Mazi Janmathep*, by Professor V. N. Naik (Bombay: Sadbhakti Publications, 1950), p. 390.

28. *CWMG*, XIV, p. 396. R. Gandhi, *Gandhi: The Man, His People, and the Empire*, p. 182.

29. Louis Fischer, *The Life of Mahatma Gandhi* (New York: Collier Books, 1962), pp. 154-55, 159.

30. Ibid., p. 159.

31. Mohandas Gandhi, "The Cult of the Bomb," *Young India*, January 2, 1930; *CWMG*, XLII, p. 363; cited by Narayan Desai, *My Life Is My Message*: II, *Satyagraha (1915-1930)* (New Delhi: Orient Blackswan, 2009), p. 560.

32. Joseph Lelyveld, *Great Soul: Mahatma Gandhi and His Struggle with India* (New York: Alfred A. Knopf, 2011), pp. 219, 320.

33. Desai, *My Life Is My Message*, II, p. 622.

34. Ibid., p. 624.

35. Ibid., p. 638.

36. Parts of this report appeared in the *Chicago Daily News*, May 22, 1930, and in Webb Miller's *I Found No Peace: The Journal of a Foreign Correspondent* (New York: Simon & Schuster, 1936), pp. 193-95; cited by Gene Sharp, *Gandhi Wields the Weapon of Moral Power: Three Case Histories* (Ahmedabad: Navajivan, 1960), pp. 138-42.

37. From an account published in *Young India* on May 29, 1930, cited by Sharp, *Gandhi Wields the Weapon of Moral Power*, p. 145.

38. M. K. Gandhi, *What Jesus Means to Me*, comp. R. K. Prabhu (Ahmedabad: Navajivan, 1959), p. 39.

39. Narayan Desai, *My Life Is My Message: IV, Svarpan (1940-1948)* (New Delhi: Orient Blackswan, 2009), p. 33.

40. Ibid., p. 46.

41. Ibid., p. 57.

42. Ibid., p. 56.

43. Narayan Desai, *The Fire and the Rose* (Ahmedabad: Navajivan, 1995), pp. 685, 688.

44. Narayan Desai has recorded the note that Gandhi wrote on July 29, 1942, after reading all five letters asking him to reconsider his fast: "'Short and Swift' does not mean at all what Mahadev contends. The issue was, to start with, a fast. Even today it is there. But that can be only if a fast is inevitable, inspired through Divine intervention where intellect has no place. But today the idea is totally irrelevant. I can ward off other doubts. I am not going into them now. All the doubts would be warded off by themselves in due course." Ibid., p. 689.

45. Ibid., p. 690.

46. Desai, *My Life Is My Message*, IV, p. 53.

47. Ibid., p. 60.

48. Ibid., p. 63.

49. Ibid., p. 62.

50. Ibid.

51. Desai, *The Fire and the Rose*, p. 7.

52. Ibid.

53. Tushar A. Gandhi, *"Let's Kill Gandhi!": A Chronicle of His Last Days, the Conspiracy, Murder, Investigation and Trial* (New Delhi: Rupa, 2007), p. 172.

54. Ibid., p. 171.

55. J. L. Kapur, *Report of Commission of Inquiry into Conspiracy to Murder Mahatma Gandhi*, part I, vol. I (New Delhi: Ministry of Home Affairs, 1970), p. 119, paragraph 9.18; p. 120, paragraph 9.21.

56. Savarkar Petition, November 14, 1913; Majumdar, *Penal Settlement in Andamans*, p. 213.

57. Savarkar, *Story of My Transportation for Life*, p. 340.

58. Ibid.

59. Ibid., p. 521.

60. Ibid., p. 556.

61. Keer, *Veer Savarkar*, pp. 163-64.

62. Savarkar, *Story of My Transportation for Life*, p. 561.

63. Ibid., p. 569.

64. Savarkar's publisher noted that the 1950 English version of *The Story of My Transportation for Life* was based on the Marathi-language second edition, published in 1947. Translator V. N. Naik then added: "The thrill and interest of the original narrative ... I have tried to retain in the [1950] English translation with such omissions and additions as the author himself has suggested to form the basis of the translation." Ibid., p. i.

65. Keer, *Veer Savarkar*, pp. 170-71.

66. Edward Luce, *In Spite of the Gods: The Strange Rise of Modern India* (New York: Doubleday, 2007), p. 151.

67. Keer, *Veer Savarkar*, p. 177.

68. Gopal Godse, *Gandhiji's Murder and After* (Delhi: Surya-Prakashan, 1989), p. 109.

69. T. A. Gandhi, *"Let's Kill Gandhi!"* p. 16.

70. Godse, *Gandhiji's Murder and After*, p. 114.

71. Keer, *Veer Savarkar*, pp. 251, 290.

72. Ibid., pp. 295, 319.

73. *Kapur Report*, Part I, Vol. I, p. 126, paragraph 10.5.

74. Pyarelal, *Mahatma Gandhi: The Last Phase*, I, Book One (Ahmedabad: Navajivan, 1956), p. 82.

75. Ibid. Savarkar's biographer, Dhananjay Keer, denied that Godse was present. Keer, *Veer Savarkar*, p. 354.

76. *CWMG*, XC, p. 408.

77. Pyarelal, *Mahatma Gandhi: The Last Phase,* II, p. 686.

78. Ibid., I, Book Two, p. 1.

79. Geoffrey Ashe, *Gandhi* (New York: Stein & Day, 1980), p. 366.

80. R. Gandhi, *Gandhi: The Man, His People, and the Empire*, p. 543.

81. Pyarelal, *Mahatma Gandhi: The Last Phase,* I, Book Two, pp. 23, 31.

82. Ibid., pp. 32-33.

83. Ibid., p. 34.

84. Ibid., pp. 34, 73-99.

85. Ibid., p. 35.

86. Dennis Dalton, *Mahatma Gandhi: Nonviolent Power in Action* (New York: Columbia University Press, 1993), p. 161.

87. Pyarelal, *Mahatma Gandhi: The Last Phase,* I, Book Two, p. 139; Payne, *Life and Death of Mahatma Gandhi*, p. 524.

88. Ibid., p. 74.

89. Payne, *Life and Death of Mahatma Gandhi*, p. 526.

90. Pyarelal, *Mahatma Gandhi: The Last Phase,* I, Book Two, p. 77.

91. Dennis Dalton has pointed out the critical role of "a device tested in Noakhali and Bihar and further developed in Calcutta: the prayer meeting. In this last phase [of Gandhi's life], almost all Gandhi's major moves and decisions, often of political import, were first announced, not at press conferences, party conventions, or political assemblies, but in prayer meetings." From Gandhi's standpoint, this was simply an expression of the fact that prayer is the heart of nonviolence. *Mahatma Gandhi: Nonviolent Power*, pp. 162-63.

92. Cited by E. Stanley Jones, *Mahatma Gandhi: An Interpretation* (Nashville: Abingdon Press, 1948), p. 102.

93. Gopal Das Khosla, *Stern Reckoning: A Survey of the Events Leading up to and following the Partition of India* (Delhi: Oxford University Press, 1989), p. 76.

94. Dalton, *Mahatma Gandhi: Nonviolent Power*, p. 162.

95. Matthew 25:40.

96. "[Hindu chauvinism's] most serious manifestation was infiltration of the Hindu middle class and even the Government services by the Rashtriya Swayamsevak Sangh (R.S.S.). It had begun to command the secret sympathy even of a section of Hindu Congressmen." Pyarelal, *Mahatma Gandhi: The Last Phase,* II, p. 687. The Hindu Mahasabha president, Dr. Shyama Prasad Mookerjee, had become a minister in Nehru's cabinet; ibid., p. 768.

97. The irony was that it was Gandhi, the man of faith, who upheld the ideal of a secular, democratic state—over against the exclusively

Muslim and Hindu visions trumpeted by Jinnah and Savarkar, whose own beliefs were secular.

98. Pyarelal, *Mahatma Gandhi: The Last Phase,* II, p. 685.

99. Rajmohan Gandhi, *Patel: A Life* (Ahmedabad: Navajivan, 1991), pp. 357-90.

100.   When the Congress Party's Working Committee met on June 14, 1947, to ratify the resolution on partition, the invited Socialist Party participant Ram Manohar Lohia observed that Gandhi "turned to Mr. Nehru and Sardar Patel in mild complaint that they had not informed him of the scheme of partition before committing themselves to it. Before Gandhiji could make his point fully, Mr. Nehru intervened with some passion to say that he had kept him fully informed. On Mahatma Gandhi's repeating that he did not know of the scheme of partition, Mr. Nehru slightly altered his earlier observation. He said that Noakhali [where Gandhi had been walking from village to village] was so far away and that, while he may not have described the details of the scheme, he had broadly written of partition to Gandhiji."

Lohia continues: "I will accept Mahatma Gandhi's version of the case, and not Mr. Nehru's, and who will not? One does not have to dismiss Mr. Nehru as a liar. All that is at issue here is whether Mahatma Gandhi knew of the scheme of partition before Mr. Nehru and Sardar Patel had committed themselves to it.... Mr. Nehru and Sardar Patel had obviously between themselves decided that it would be best not to scare Gandhiji away before the deed was definitely resolved upon....

"Messrs. Nehru and Patel were offensively aggressive to Gandhiji at this meeting.... What appeared to be astonishing then, as now, though I can today understand it somewhat better, was the exceedingly rough behaviour of these two chosen disciples towards their master. There was something psychopathic about it. They seemed to have set their heart on something and, whenever they scented that Gandhiji was preparing to obstruct them, they barked violently"; Ram Manohar Lohia, *Guilty Men of India's Partition* (New Delhi: Rupa, 2008), pp. 23-25.

101.   Godse, *Gandhiji's Murder and After,* p. 172.

102.   Narayan Apte's notes for a speech at Nagar, found among his personal papers; cited by K. L. Gauba, *The Assassination of Mahatma Gandhi* (Bombay: Jaico, 1969), p. 80.

103.   Deposition of Digambar R. Badge, Approver, in *Printed Record of Mahatma Gandhi Murder Case* (in U.S. Library of Congress Law Library), I, p. 82. In the 1948 trial held at Red Fort, Delhi, for the assassination of Gandhi, arms salesman Digambar Badge testi-

fied as an "approver," providing state's evidence against his co-conspirators in return for the dismissal of charges against him. In his judgment, Judge Atma Charan found Badge a credible witness, subject to the standard legal requirement of corroborative evidence. The judge stated, "The examination and the cross-examination of the approver went on from July 20, 1948, until July 30, 1948. He was cross-examined for nearly seven days. There was thus an ample opportunity to observe his demeanor and the manner of his giving evidence. He gave his version of the facts in a direct and straightforward manner. He did not evade cross-examination or attempt to evade or fence with any question. It would not have been possible for anyone to have given evidence so unfalteringly stretching over such a long period and with such particularity in regard to facts which had never taken place. It is difficult to conceive of anyone memorizing so long and so detailed a story if altogether without foundation." Judge Atma Charan ruled that corroborative evidence was lacking only in Badge's testimony regarding defendant Vinayak D. Savarkar (Judgment of the Special Judge, Red Fort, Delhi, Vol. III, ibid., pp. 89, 90). The three appeals judges also set aside the trial judge's convictions of Shankar Kistayya, Badge's servant, and Dr. Dattatraya S. Parchure, who was accused of helping to procure the pistol Godse used (Judgment of the Full Bench in Mahatma Gandhi Murder Case, pp. 196, 558-59). The high-court justices decided that Kistayya had merely acted as Badge's servant, not an accomplice, and that Parchure's confession had not been voluntary (T. A. Gandhi, "Let's Kill Gandhi!" p. 727). As we shall see, the Kapur Commission, which reviewed Gandhi's assassination in 1970, found that the government possessed corroborative evidence against Savarkar but failed to present it at the trial.

104. Manohar Malgonkar, *The Men Who Killed Gandhi* (New Delhi: Orient, 1981), pp. 25, 77.

105. *CWMG*, XC, p. 417.

106. Badge Deposition, p. 82.

107. Ibid., p. 84. The extent to which Gandhi's loving nonviolence affected even his assassins can be seen by their repeated use of the affectionate, honorific term "Gandhiji" to identify the man they intended to kill. Because his assassins continued to feel his love, they were unable to regard him in a personal sense as their enemy. They killed him for ideological reasons, but even so, were unable to objectify him as a man who thought evil of them. Godse echoing Savarkar claimed wrongly, but with an element of respect in his references to his target, "To my

mind Gandhiji himself was the greatest supporter and advocate of Pakistan and no power could have any control on him in this attitude of his. In these circumstances the only effective remedy to relieve the Hindus from the Muslim atrocities was, *to my mind* [emphasis added], to remove Gandhiji from this world." From the courtroom statement of Nathuram Godse, *May It Please Your Honour* (Delhi: Surya Bharti Prakashan, 1987), p. 152.

Because even those who killed Gandhi felt his love, they knew he was (and would remain in death) "Gandhiji." For Godse to bow to Gandhi when he shot him to death was therefore not simply a hypocritical ploy. Believing that he *had* to kill him, Godse knew nevertheless that "Gandhiji," who was at the same time bowing to him, loved him.

108.   Dalton, *Mahatma Gandhi: Nonviolent Power*, p. 146.

109.   Payne, *Life and Death of Mahatma Gandhi*, p. 533.

110.   Pyarelal, *Mahatma Gandhi: The Last Phase,* I, Book Two (Ahmedabad: Navajivan, 1966), p. 7. In a careful analysis of the "Great Calcutta Killing," Dennis Dalton observed: "the crux of the [Hindu] indictment [was] Suhrawardy's failure to take adequate preventive measures." Dalton, *Mahatma Gandhi: Nonviolent Power*, p. 146.

111.   Pyarelal, *Mahatma Gandhi: The Last Phase,* I, Book Two, pp. 7-8.

112.   Ibid., p. 336.

113.   Ibid., p. 104

114.   Nirmal Kumar Bose, *My Days with Gandhi* (New Delhi: Orient Longman, 1974), p. 198.

115.   Ibid., pp. 198-99.

116.   Ibid., p. 200.

117.   Pyarelal, *Mahatma Gandhi: The Last Phase,* II, p. 364.

118.   Bose, *My Days with Gandhi*, p.224.

119.   Rajmohan Gandhi, *The Good Boatman: A Portrait of Gandhi* (New Delhi: Penguin Books India, 1997), p. 350.

120.   Ibid., p. 351.

121.   Pyarelal, *Mahatma Gandhi: The Last Phase*, II, p. 367.

122.   Dalton, *Mahatma Gandhi: Nonviolent Power*, p. 152.

123.   Pyarelal, *Mahatma Gandhi: The Last Phase*, II, p. 369.

124.   Manubehn Gandhi, *The Miracle of Calcutta* (Ahmedabad: Navajivan, 1959), p. 66.

125.   *CWMG*, LXXXIX, p. 130.

126.   Pyarelal, *Mahatma Gandhi: The Last Phase*, II, p. 404.

127.   Dalton, *Mahatma Gandhi: Nonviolent Power*, p. 154.

128. *CWMG*, LXXXIX, pp. 129-32.

129. Pyarelal, *Mahatma Gandhi: The Last Phase,* II, p. 409.

130. Ibid., p. 421.

131. Ibid.

132. Desai, *My Life Is My Message,* IV, p. 433.

133. Pyarelal, *Mahatma Gandhi: The Last Phase,* II, p. 423.

134. Desai, *My Life Is My Message,* IV, p. 435.

135. Pyarelal, *Mahatma Gandhi: The Last Phase,* II, p. 424.

136. Letter from Gandhi to Suhrawardy, October 27, 1947; *CWMG,* LXXXIX, p. 418.

137. M. Waheeduzzaman Manik, "Huseyn Shaheed Suhrawardy: Glimpses of His Political Struggle," *The Daily Star: Internet Edition,* December 5, 2007.

138. Ibid.

139. Ibid.

140. "Huseyn Shaheed Suhrawardy," *Wikipedia.*

141. Mohammad H. R. Talukdar, ed., *Memoirs of Huseyn Shaheed Suhrawardy with a Brief Account of His Life and Work* (Karachi: Oxford University Press, 2009), p. 71.

142. Ibid.

143. *Kapur Report*, Part I, Vol. II, p. 221, paragraph 12H.20A.

144. Badge Deposition, p. 84.

145. Pyarelal, *Mahatma Gandhi: The Last Phase,* II, p. 711.

146. *CWMG,* XC, pp. 428-29.

147. Pyarelal, *Mahatma Gandhi: The Last Phase,* II, p. 718.

148. Ibid., p. 719.

149. Ibid., p. 720.

150. Fischer, *Life of Mahatma Gandhi*, p. 495.

151. Pyarelal, *Mahatma Gandhi: The Last Phase,* II, pp. 722-23.

152. Badge Deposition, p. 85; T. A. Gandhi, *"Let's Kill Gandhi!"* p. 960.

153. Ibid.

154. Ibid.

155. Pyarelal, *Mahatma Gandhi: The Last Phase,* II, p. 726.

156. Ibid., p. 727.

157. Ibid., p. 728.

158. Manuben Gandhi, *Last Glimpses of Bapu* (Delhi: Shiva Lal Agarwala, 1962), p. 190.

159. Pyarelal, *Mahatma Gandhi: The Last Phase,* II, p. 730.

160. Manuben Gandhi, *Last Glimpses*, p. 192.

161. Pyarelal, *Mahatma Gandhi: The Last Phase*, II, p. 730.

162. Ibid., p. 731. Manuben Gandhi, *Last Glimpses*, p. 199.

163. *CWMG*, XC, pp. 452-53.

164. Badge Deposition, p. 87.

165. Ibid.

166. Ibid.

167. Ibid.

168. Ibid.

169. *Kapur Report*, Part I, Vol. I, p. 58, paragraph 5.10.

170. Ibid.

171. Badge Deposition, p. 90.

172. Ibid.

173. Manuben Gandhi, *Last Glimpses*, p. 218.

174. M. K. Gandhi, *Delhi Diary: Prayer Speeches from September 10, 1947, to January 30, 1948* (Ahmedabad: Navajivan, 1948), p. 357.

175. Ibid.

176. Manuben Gandhi, *Last Glimpses*, p. 219.

177. Ibid. *CWMG*, XC, p. 464.

178. T. A. Gandhi, *"Let's Kill Gandhi!"* p. 94.

179. Manuben Gandhi, *Last Glimpses*, p. 223.

180. Ibid., p. 222.

181. Ibid.

182. Pyarelal, *Mahatma Gandhi: The Last Phase*, II, p. 750.

183. G. D. Khosla, *The Murder of the Mahatma and Other Cases from a Judge's Notebook* (Bombay: Jaico, 1968), p. 245. Prosecution Exhibit 127, "Daily Hindu Rashtra," *Printed Record of Mahatma Gandhi Murder Case*, VII, p. 2.

184. "Investigation at Delhi," *Kapur Report*, Part II, Vol. V, pp. 185-239.

185. Ibid., p. 189.

186. Ibid., pp. 189, 215, 232.

187. Ibid., p. 205.

188. Ibid., p. 190.

189. Ibid., pp. 125, 126, 236.

190. Dr. Jagdish Chandra Jain, *I Could Not Save Bapu* (Kamacha, Banares: Jagran Sahitya Mandir, no date), pp. 13, 16.

191. Ibid., p. 21.

192. Ibid., p. 12.

193. *Kapur Report*, Part II, Vol. IV, p. 7, paragraph 18.29.

194. Deposition of Morarji R. Desai, *Mahatma Gandhi Murder Case*, I, p. 167.

195. Morarji Desai said that he "gave [Patel] the necessary information in regard to what I had been told by Professor Jain and the action taken by me." Ibid. However, three witnesses to the Kapur Commission who had worked closely with Patel (then deceased), including his secretary, V. Shankar, said they had no knowledge then of Jain's story or of Desai's sharing it with Patel at Ahmedabad. *Kapur Report*, Part II, Vol. V, pp. 124, paragraph 21.7; 126, paragraphs 21.16-17; 127, paragraph 21.25.

196. Pyarelal, *Mahatma Gandhi: The Last Phase*, II, p. 756.

197. Ibid.

198. Ibid.

199. Rohini Kumar Chaudhury, MP, to Hon. Sardar Vallabhbhai Patel, February 6, 1948, cited and translated from Hindi by T. A. Gandhi, *"Let's Kill Gandhi!"* p. 529.

200. According to police testimony to the Kapur Commission, prior to the January 20 bombing incident, there were at Birla House "one Head Constable and one Foot Constable in the prayer grounds. There were at the main gate of the Birla House one head Constable and four Constables.... After the bomb incident, the number of policemen was immediately increased to one Assistant Sub-Inspector, two Head Constables, and sixteen Foot Constables. In addition to this, there were plain-clothes policemen, one Sub-Inspector, four Head Constables, and two Foot Constables who were all armed with revolvers." *Kapur Report*, Part I, Vol. II, p. 207, paragraphs 12.G.2-3.

201. Manuben Gandhi, *Last Glimpses*, p. 224.

202. Ibid., p. 225.

203. *Kapur Report*, Part II, Vol. V, p. 136, paragraph 21.60.

204. T. A. Gandhi, *"Let's Kill Gandhi!"* p. 138.

205. *Kapur Report*, Part II, Vol. V, pp. 223-24, paragraph 23.173.

206. Ibid., p. 224, paragraph 23.173.

207. Bombay's Deputy Police Commissioner J. D. Nagarvala said he conducted his investigation under the theory that there was a gang whose objective was "one of kidnapping Mahatma Gandhi and not of murder." Ibid., Part II, Vol. IV, p. 31, paragraph 18.127. The Kapur Commission found Nagarvala's kidnapping theory "so astounding" in its misinterpretation of the evidence that it could only attribute it to the possibility of a faulty understanding of the Punjabi lan-

guage by Nagarvala's contacts and informers. Ibid., p. 45, paragraph 18.201.

208. Ibid., Part II, Vol. VI, p. 305, paragraph 25.113.

209. Ibid., Part II, Vol. V, p. 209, paragraph 23.109.

210. Ibid., Part I, Vol. III, p. 278, paragraph 15.113.

211. Ibid., paragraph 15.115.

212. The Kapur Commission could make no sense of U. H. Rana's decision to take such an indirect train route across India on a mission that might have saved Gandhi's life. The *Kapur Report* also wondered why Inspector General Sanjevi did not assign the mission in the first place to an officer who could go by air to Bombay, reaching the destination much more quickly. Rana said it was because Sanjevi "did not think that the conspirators would act so swiftly." Ibid. A strange lack of urgency seemed to have infected all the key police officers with the task of pursuing the conspirators against Gandhi. *Kapur Report*, Part I, Vol. I, p. 28, paragraphs 341-42.

213. Ibid., Part II, Vol. V, p. 185, paragraph 23.2; Vol. VI, p. 318, paragraph 25.173.

214. Ibid., Part I, Vol. III, p. 284, paragraph 15.144.

215. Ibid., Part II, Vol. IV, p. 30, paragraph 18.125.

216. Ibid., Part II, Vol. V, p. 216, paragraph 23.141.

217. Ibid., p. 214, paragraph 23.135.

218. Ibid., P. 221, paragraph 23.164.

219. Ibid., Part II, Vol. VI, p. 305, paragraph 25.113. "The object of watching Savarkar's house [Nagarvala said] was to see who were visiting him. He added that he did not detain [members of the] Savarkar group before the murder because it would have caused not only commotion but upheaval in the Maharashtrian Region." Ibid., Part II, Vol. IV, p. 37, paragraph 18.155. This extension of Nagarvala's comment from Savarkar himself to the group of conspirators visiting him is an implicit admission that the Bombay police knew they were coming and going; they observed the same deference toward Savarkar's henchmen as they did to the master.

220. Vincent Sheean, *Lead Kindly Light* (New York: Random House, 1949), p. 168.

221. Ibid., pp. 183-85. Emphasis in original.

222. This paragraph was completed with the help of Roger Ludwig and Bert Sacks in their critiques. Roger emphasized the paradox of Gandhi drawing power from the poorest people he met. Bert added the thought: "You might want to draw this out by including those people

who commit acts of violent cruelty. It seems to me that Gandhi's relation to General Smuts of South Africa and to Godse and even Savarkar is at the heart of his nonviolence and truth-force. (And the most difficult challenge to many of us!)"

As Bert says, Gandhi saw God face to face not only in the poorest but, above all, in those who were most committed to frustrating his will "by acts of violent cruelty." In addition to Smuts, Godse, and Savarkar, we can add the two political leaders who, in terms of their power and dedication, proved to be the greatest obstacles to the realization of Gandhi's nonviolent vision: Winston Churchill and Muhammad Ali Jinnah. Gandhi never ceased loving them. That meant extending his friendship and support to the two men who were, however blindly, standing in the way of Gandhi's vision of a nonviolent world, realized through India as a catalyst of nonviolent transformation.

Churchill was offended by the idea of even negotiating with Gandhi, as he said in a famous comment: "It is alarming and also nauseating to see Mr. Gandhi, a seditious Middle Temple lawyer now posing as a fakir of a type well-known in the East, striding half-naked up the steps of the Vice-regal palace, while he is still organizing and conducting a campaign of civil disobedience, to parley on equal terms with the representative of the King-Emperor. Such a spectacle can only increase the unrest in India and the danger to which white people there are exposed." Arthur Herman, *Gandhi & Churchill* (New York: Bantam Books, 2008), p. 359.

While Gandhi was imprisoned under Churchill's World War II government, he wrote a good-humored, four-sentence-long letter reaching out to the man who wanted to destroy him (ibid. p. 538):

Dear Prime Minister,

You are reported to have a desire to crush the simple "Naked Fakir" as you are said to have described me. I have been long trying to be a Fakir and that naked—a more difficult task. I therefore regard the expression as a compliment, however unintended. I approach you then as such and ask you to trust and use me for the sake of your people and mine and through them those of the world.

Your sincere friend,
M. K. Gandhi

After Gandhi was released and learned that his captors had never sent the letter to Churchill, he made it public. However, Churchill was not interested in Gandhi's offer to be used by him for the sake of Britain, India, and the world.

In spite of Muhammad Ali Jinnah's total dedication to dividing India to create Pakistan, Gandhi, without compromising his own vision, became Jinnah's advocate in negotiations with the British. To the astonishment of Viceroy Lord Louis Mountbatten, Gandhi proposed to him in April 1947 that Jinnah be offered the office of prime minister of the independent state of India. Gandhi sought in that unique way to overcome the impasse between Muslim and Hindu demands that were threatening to tear India apart—by giving Jinnah the leadership of all of India.

"The selection of the Cabinet," Gandhi proposed, " should be "left entirely to Mr. Jinnah," who would have to stipulate on behalf of its members that "they will do their utmost to preserve peace throughout India."

"If Mr. Jinnah accepted this offer," Gandhi said, "the Congress would guarantee to cooperate freely and sincerely, so long as all the measures that Mr. Jinnah's Cabinet bring forward are in the interests of the Indian people as a whole. The sole referee of what is or is not in the interests of India as a whole will be Lord Mountbatten, in his personal capacity" (*CWMG*, LXXXVII, p. 199).

Mountbatten wrote in a report that the mahatma's ingenious scheme to break the deadlock between Gandhi's Congress Party and Jinnah's Muslim League "staggered me. I asked, 'what would Mr. Jinnah say to such a proposal?' The reply was 'If you tell him I am the author, he will reply, "Wily Gandhi."' I [Mountbatten] then remarked, 'And I presume Mr. Jinnah will be right?' To which [Gandhi] replied with great fervour, 'No, I am entirely sincere in my suggestion'" (cited by Stanley Wolpert, *Jinnah of Pakistan* [New York: Oxford University Press, 1984], p. 316).

Mountbatten did convey Gandhi's proposal to Nehru, who was shocked by his teacher's way to resolve the Hindu-Muslim crisis, which would have meant disrupting Nehru's own rise to power. Nehru and other Congress Party leaders whose power was similarly threatened by Gandhi's proposal worked to convince Mountbatten of its impracticality, and did. Mountbatten never raised the offer to Jinnah, although the viceroy thought it quite possible Jinnah would have accepted (ibid., p. 319).

Gandhi never stopped believing in his most bitter opponents' abilities to act on their own truths in redemptive ways. His belief in them was at the heart of his nonviolence.

223. Sheean, *Lead Kindly Light*, pp. 185-87, 189.
224. Ibid., p. 191.

225. Ibid.
226. Ibid., p. 193.
227. Ibid., p. 17.
228. Ibid., p. 16.
229. Pyarelal, *Mahatma Gandhi: The Last Phase*, II, p. 767.
230. Ibid., p. 766.
231. Ibid., p. 768.
232. Ibid.
233. Ibid., p. 769.
234. Ibid., p. 772. Manuben Gandhi, *Last Glimpses*, p. 306.
235. Manuben Gandhi, *Last Glimpses*, p. 308.
236. Ibid., p. 309.
237. Pyarelal, *Mahatma Gandhi: The Last Phase*, II, p. 773. Pyarelal adds in a note: "After a most careful and exhaustive inquiry from first witnesses on the spot that I made at the time, I am convinced that the last words that issued from Gandhiji's mouth as he lost consciousness were not 'Hey Rama!' but 'Rama, Rama'—not an invocation but simple remembrance of the Name" (ibid., p. 861 n. 5).
238. Sheean, *Lead Kindly Light*, pp. 203-4.
239. Dalton, *Mahatma Gandhi: Nonviolent Power*, p. 167.
240. Cited by T. A. Gandhi. *"Let's Kill Gandhi!"* pp. 138-39.
241. Ibid., pp. xviii, 139.
242. G. K. Handoo to the Kapur Commission, *Kapur Report*, Part I, Vol. II, p. 221, paragraph 12H.19; p. 222, paragraph 12H.23.
243. Ibid., p. 221, paragraph 12H.20; p. 222, paragraph 12H.23.
244. Manuben Gandhi, *Last Glimpses*, p. 225.
245. P. L. Inamdar, *The Story of the Red Fort Trial 1948-49* (Bombay: Popular Prakashan, 1979), p. 142.
246. Ibid., p. 141.
247. Godse, *May It Please Your Honour*, p. 60.
248. Inamdar, *Story of the Red Fort Trial*, p. 142.
249. Ibid., p. 141.
250. T. A. Gandhi, *"Let's Kill Gandhi!"* p. 607.
251. Godse, *May It Please Your Honour*, p. 154.
252. Ibid.
253. Ibid., p. 42.
254. Ibid., p. 51.
255. What the judge had given Godse, by letting him deliver his nine-hour speech against Gandhi, the government then took away by banning its publication. The government realized the judge had gone

too far in his permissiveness toward Godse, tilting the politics of the case too much in favor of the murderers. The ban on the speech's publication was overturned three decades later (Gopal Godse's introduction to *May It Please Your Honour*, p. 20). In the meantime, the government's suppression of the statement had helped give it a legendary status among Savarkar's ideological heirs, who celebrated Nathuram Godse as a martyr and Savarkar as a great teacher.

256. *Kapur Report*, Part II, Vol. VI, p. 317, paragraphs 25.161 and 25.166; p. 318, paragraphs 25.168, 25.170, and 25.173.

257. Ibid., p. 318, paragraph 25.173.

258. Ibid., Part I, Vol. I, p. 36, paragraph 3.58.

259. Ibid.

260. Ibid., Part II, Vol. VI, p. 303, paragraph 25.106.

261. Letter from Patel to Nehru, February 27, 1948. *Sardar Patel's Correspondence 1945-50*, VI, ed. Durga Das (Ahmedabad: Navajivan, 1973), p. 56.

262. The government kept Savarkar's employees, Appa Ramchandra Kasar and Gajanan Vishnu Damle, in prison for over two years, through the Gandhi murder trial and appeals. They were never called to testify. When they were finally released, Savarkar did not welcome them back. Savarkar's biographer writes that Kasar and Damle "were unceremoniously asked to care for themselves." Keer, *Veer Savarkar*, p. 478.

263. Lourenco De Salvador, *Who Killed Gandhi?* (Lisbon, Portugal: printed privately, no date), p. 149.

264. Noorani, *Savarkar and Hindutva*, p. 130.

265. Ibid.

266. Noorani's citation of Morarji Desai's testimony is drawn from *The Times of India* of September 1, 1948, which "carried the text of the Chief Prosecutive Counsel, C. K. Daphtary's application to Judge Atma Charan the previous day" (ibid., pp. 130-31). Desai recalled vaguely in his 1979 autobiography the courtroom exchange: "Shri Savarkar's lawyer put me a question, the details of which I have forgotten, but I have the impression that it related to my personal belief in the matter. The Judge told me that I was not bound to answer that question. But I told the Judge that I had no objection to answering the question and requested him to ask the accused whether the latter really wanted a specific reply. If he so desired, I was prepared to answer. When I said this the lawyer retracted his question and did not cross-examine me further." Morarji Desai, *The Story of My Life*, I (Oxford:

Pergamon Press, 1979), pp. 269-70. However, the question withdrawn by Savarkar did not relate to Desai's "personal belief in the matter," as he recalled, but rather (as Savarkar's lawyer realized almost too late by Desai's warning response) "the full facts" the government possessed on Savarkar as a conspirator in Gandhi's assassination.

267. T. A. Gandhi, *"Let's Kill Gandhi!"* pp. 732-33.

268. "Publisher's Note," opening page in Vinayak Damodar Savarkar, *Six Glorious Epochs of Indian History* (New Delhi: Rajdhani Granthagar, 1971).

269. Ibid., p. 78.

270. Ibid.

271. Ibid., p. 76.

272. David Hardiman, *Gandhi in His Time and Ours: The Global Legacy of His Ideas* (New York: Columbia University Press, 2003), pp. 174-75.

273. Savarkar, *Story of My Transportation for Life*, p. 521.

274. Ibid.

275. Ibid., p. 569.

276. Luce, *In Spite of the Gods*, pp. 143-44. Even the RSS's second-place size of two million relative to the Chinese Communist Party is based on a low estimate. Some observers place its membership nearer six million. The RSS manages to be both huge and secretive. It keeps its membership rolls private (ibid., p. 143).

277. Ibid., pp. 143-44.

278. Arundhati Roy has described how the BJP put into practice Savarkar's ideology of Hindutva in a successful bid for power: "In 1990, [the BJP's] leader, L. K. Advani, traveled across the country whipping up hatred against Muslims and demanding that the Babri Masjid, an old sixteenth-century mosque that stood on a disputed site in Ayodhya, be demolished and a Ram temple built in its place. In 1992, a mob, egged on by Advani, demolished the mosque. In early 1993, a mob rampaged through Mumbai attacking Muslims, killing almost one thousand people. As revenge, a series of bomb blasts ripped through the city, killing about two hundred and fifty people. Feeding off the communal frenzy it had generated, the BJP, which had only two seats in Parliament in 1984, defeated the Congress Party in 1998 and came to power at the center." Arundhati Roy, *Field Notes on Democracy: Listening to Grasshoppers* (Chicago: Haymarket Books, 2009), p. 9.

279. Luce, *In Spite of the Gods*, p. 148.

280. Noorani, *Savarkar and Hindutva*, p. 1.

281. Ibid., p. 6.

282. R. Gandhi, *The Man, His People, and the Empire*, p. 662.

283. Cited by George Perkovich in *India's Nuclear Bomb: The Impact on Global Proliferation* (Berkeley: University of California Press, 1999), p. 14.

284. Ibid., p. 20.

285. Ibid., p. 18.

286. Cited by Perkovich, *India's Nuclear Bomb*, p. 20.

287. Cited by John Dear, *Mohandas Gandhi: Essential Writings* (Maryknoll, NY: Orbis Books, 2002), p. 143.

288. "On April 2, 1954, Prime Minister Nehru proposed 'some sort of ... stand-still agreement in respect, at least, of these actual [nuclear] explosions, even if arrangements about the discontinuance of production and stockpiling must await more substantial agreements among those principally concerned." William Epstein, *The Last Chance: Nuclear Proliferation and Arms Control* (New York: Free Press, 1976), pp. 48-49, 225.

289. Perkovich, *India's Nuclear Bomb*, p. 35. In a 1960 conversation with "the top military official in the U.S. nuclear establishment," Major General (ret.) Kenneth D. Nichols, Prime Minister Nehru, and his AEC chairman Homi Bhabha expressed a "more candid ambivalence" regarding India's weapons capability. General Nichols reported that in their conversation, Nehru abruptly asked Bhabha,

> "Can you develop an atomic bomb?" Bhabha assured him that he could and in reply to Nehru's next question about time, he estimated that he would need about a year to do it. I was really astounded to be hearing these questions from the one I thought to be one of the world's most peace-loving leaders.
>
> He then asked me if I agreed with Bhabha, and I replied that I knew of no reason why Bhabha could not do it. He had men who were as qualified or more qualified than our young scientists were fifteen years earlier. [Nehru] concluded by saying to Bhabha, "Well, don't do it, until I tell you to." Ibid., p. 36.

290. Ibid.

291. Ibid., pp. 13-40.

292. Stanley Wolpert, *Gandhi's Passion: The Life and Legacy of Mahatma Gandhi* (New York: Oxford University Press, 2001), p. 261.

293. Canadian non-proliferation expert William Epstein thought India's nuclear explosion under the Rajasthan desert on May 18, 1974, changed the rules of nuclear non-proliferation. Epstein wrote: "The

Rajasthan test proved that a relatively poor developing country could use atomic fission for an underground explosion (somewhat more complicated than one in the atmosphere) that had definite potential for warlike purposes.... There is no essential difference between the technology of a nuclear explosion intended for peaceful applications and that of one intended for waging nuclear war.... The bombs that destroyed Hiroshima and Nagasaki were about the same size as the Indian device—between 15 and 20 kilotons in explosive yield." Epstein, *The Last Chance*, p. 221.

294. *Hind Swaraj*, p. 163.

Gandhi, Godse, and the Cross

1. G. K. Handoo, official in charge of security for Prime Minister Nehru, in his testimony to the Kapur Commission, *Kapur Report*, Part I, Vol. II, p. 221, paragraph 12H.19; p. 222, paragraph 12H.23.

2. "Investigation at Delhi," *Kapur Report*, Part II, Vol. V, p. 125, paragraph 21.13; p. 126, paragraph 21.18; p. 236, paragraph 23.243.

3. A. G. Noorani, *Savarkar and Hindutva: The Godse Connection* (New Delhi: Left Word Books, 2002), p. 130.

4. The United States government's National Security Council directive 10/2, issued on June 18, 1948, sanctioned covert operations such as propaganda, sabotage, economic warfare, and assassinations to achieve victory in the Cold War against communism. According to NSC 10/2, the condition for these covert activities by U.S. agencies, coordinated by the CIA, was that they be "so planned and executed that ... if uncovered the US government can plausibly disclaim any responsibility for them." The CIA's master of plausible deniability was its long-time director, Allen Dulles, from whose biography, *Gentleman Spy* by Peter Grose (New York: Houghton Mifflin, 1994), p. 293, NSC 10/2 is cited. Allen Dulles and his CIA hierarchy covertly used intermediaries known as "cut-outs" to distance themselves from assassinations and other covert operations they could then plausibly deny. A cut-out's reward would often, in the end, be similar to the target's, as Lieutenant General Hoyt S. Vandenburg, then head of the Central Intelligence Group, explained to a House Committee on Expenditures in 1947: "if [a cut-out] gets in trouble, we wash our hands of it. For that reason, his pay has got to be fairly good, because his throat is cut and we wash our hands of him, and we say we know nothing about him" (cited by Grose,

Gentleman Spy, p. 277). Savarkar was a master of plausible deniability from London to Delhi, with more limited resources and less of a shield than the CIA director had.

5. Nathuram Godse, *May It Please Your Honour* (Delhi: Surya Bharti Prakashan, 1987), pp. 42, 55.

6. Deposition of Digambar R. Badge, Approver, in *Printed Record of Mahatma Gandhi Murder Case* (in U.S. Library of Congress Law Library), I, p. 84.

7. Godse, *May It Please Your Honour*, p. 98.

8. Ibid., p. 111.

9. Ibid., pp. 113-14.

10. Ibid., p. 114.

11. Ibid., p. 115.

12. Ibid., pp. 130-31.

13. Ibid., p. 131.

14. Ibid., pp. 131-32.

15. M. K. Gandhi, "The Jesus I Love," in *What Jesus Means to Me* (Ahmedabad: Navajivan, 1959), pp. 13-16.

16. John S. Hoyland, "Gandhi's Satyagraha and the Way of the Cross," in *Mahatma Gandhi: Essays and Reflections on His Life and Work*, ed. S. Radhakrishnan (Bombay: Jaico, 1956), p. 98. In a separate description of this meeting, Pyarelal reported that Gandhi's visitors were in India to attend the International Missionary Conference that opened on December 12, 1938. Pyarelal's entry in the *Collected Works of Mahatma Gandhi* (Electronic Book) LXXIV: September 9, 1938–January 29, 1939 (dated "before December 12, 1938") is titled "Discussion with Christian Missionaries."

17. Hoyland, "Gandhi's Satyagraha."

18. Ibid., pp. 98-99.

19. Ibid., p. 100.

20. Vincent Sheean, *Lead Kindly Light* (New York: Random House, 1949), pp. 186, 189.

21. Hoyland, "Gandhi's Satyagraha," p. 102.

22. Ibid., p. 105.

23. Ibid., p. 107. Gandhi reportedly cited five stanzas from Percy Bysshe Shelley's poem, *Mask of Anarchy*:

> Stand ye calm and resolute
> Like a forest close and mute,

With folded arms and looks which are
Weapons of unvanquished war.

And if then the tyrants dare,
Let them ride among you there,
Slash, and stab, and maim, and hew—
What they like, that let them do.

With folded arms and steady eyes,
And little fear, and less surprise,
Look upon them as they slay,
Till their rage has died away.

Then they will return with shame
To the place from which they came,
And the blood thus shed will speak
In hot blushes on their cheek.

Rise like lions after slumber
In unvanquishable number—
Shake your chains to earth, like dew
Which in sleep has fallen on you—
Ye are many, they are few.

24. Ibid., p. 114.

25. Ibid., p. 115. The remarkable story of Abdul Ghaffar Khan, Gandhi's great Muslim disciple, and his *Khudai Khidmatgars* ("Servants of God") has been told by (1) D. G. Tendulkar, *Abdul Ghaffar Khan: Faith Is a Battle* (Bombay: Popular Prakashan, 1967); (2) Eknath Easwaran, *Nonviolent Soldier of Islam: Badshah Khan, A Man to Match His Mountains* (Tomales, CA: Nilgiri Press, 1999).

26. Martin Luther King, Jr., "Where Do We Go from Here?" in *A Testament of Hope: The Essential Writings of Martin Luther King, Jr.*, ed. James M. Washington (San Francisco: Harper & Row, 1986), p. 252.

27. Martin Luther King, Jr., "Pilgrimage to Nonviolence," in *A Testament of Hope*, p. 39.

Index